THE BIBLICAL FAMILY

the Biblical Family

V. PAUL MARSTON

Cornerstone Books • Westchester, Illinois

Bible quotations are taken from the *Revised Standard Version* (RSV) or the *New International Version* (NIV), unless otherwise stated.

Citation of multitudes of reference works can become tedious to read, and we have usually restricted such citation to three of the most generally accepted works: *The New International Dictionary of New Testament Theology*, vols. 1-3, 1975-1978, Colin Brown, ed.; *Theological Dictionary of the New Testament*, vols. 1-10, 1964-1977, G. Kittel and G. Friedrich, eds.; *A Greek-English Lexicon* (ninth edition), H. G. Liddell and R. Scott (revised by M. S. Jones and R. McKenzie).

To establish points of background and/or linguistics, reference may also be made to the following: *The Septuagint* (LXX): The Greek version of the Old Testament used in apostolic days. This includes parts of Apocryphal writings generally not accepted by evangelicals as inspired, but helpful for background. *The Mishnah and Talmud:* The Mishnah contains second-century written versions of rabbinical traditions, some of which go back to before the time of Christ. The Talmud is a later commentary on these. *Josephus and Philo:* A Jewish historian and a philosopher of the first century. *Pagan writers:* Works of Plato, Aristotle, Menander, etc. give useful background. *Early Christian epistles:* Letters of Clement, Ignatius, and Polycarp reflect the early Christians' viewpoint.

Copyright © 1980 by V. Paul Marston. Published by Cornerstone Books, a division of Good News Publishers, Westchester, Illinois 60153. All rights reserved. No part of this publication may be reproduced, stored in a retrieval system or transmitted in any form by any means, electronic, mechanical, photocopy, recording, or otherwise, without the prior permission of the publisher, except as provided in USA copyright law.
Printed in the United States of America.
Library of Congress Catalog Card Number 80-68332.
ISBN 0-89107-192-X.

My sincere thanks are due to my friend and coauthor Roger T. Forster, who collaborated on the first drafts of this work. Thanks are also due to other friends, particularly Stephen Gaukroger, for helpful comment. My greatest debt is owed to my own family, who daily teach me of family relationships.

Contents

Prologue	Discovering True Humanity	9
Chapter 1	On Being Human	15
Chapter 2	The Basis of Marriage	23
Chapter 3	Dating and Choosing a Partner	31
Chapter 4	Marriage and Wedding	39
Chapter 5	The Purpose of Sex	49
Chapter 6	Sex and Purity of Mind	60
Chapter 7	Headship and Subjection in Marriage	71
Chapter 8	Male and Female in Marriage	80
Chapter 9	Family Relationships	94
Chapter 10	Men and Women in the Church Family	105
Chapter 11	Marriage Problems and Divorce	124
Chapter 12	The Single Person	144
Appendix 1	Homosexual Relationships	151
Appendix 2	Paul on Dressing for Church	165
Appendix 3	Women as Coheirs	171
Notes		182
Works Cited or Referred to		201
Further Reading		202

PROLOGUE

Discovering True Humanity

Reading: 2 Timothy 3:1—4:5

> In the last days there will come times of stress. For men will be lovers of self, lovers of money, proud, arrogant, abusive, disobedient to their parents, ungrateful, unholy, inhuman, implacable, slanderers, profligates, fierce, haters of good, treacherous, reckless, swollen with conceit, lovers of pleasure rather than lovers of God, holding the form of religion but denying the power of it.[1]

Thus the Apostle Paul censured nominally religious people who behave wrongly in their relationships with others. Whether his words apply more to our generation than to previous ones is beyond us to determine. The world, after all, has always had to endure religious people whose behavior reflects a lack of genuine faith.

Our times may or may not be marked by more wrong *behavior;* but they surely are marked by more debate about the delineation between what *is* wrong and what is merely a matter of custom or personal taste. Of course, thinking people have always recognized that *some* norms of any society are merely social custom, and deviations from such norms have no real moral significance. But there are those today who claim that many life-styles departing radically from the norm should likewise be regarded as matters of unusual personal taste rather than as moral issues. "Why," they ask, "should we assume that the only right form of family life is a nuclear family of father, mother and children? Why not group marriage? Temporary alliance? Homosexual marriage? Might not adultery actually improve a marriage?" Other issues are raised by those in the women's liberation movement, who claim that much traditional thinking about marriage is based on a myth of male supremacy. "No self-respecting modern woman," they say, "could agree to accept a husband as head of the house, or give up all her rights to a career of her own."

What is the Christian to make of all this? A few, professing Christianity but wanting to join the "liberty" bandwagon, have abandoned virtually all standards except a vague banner of "love." Others, frightened by the tide of change, have clung tenaciously to a narrow patriarchal system which they were taught in their youth as "proper" family life, denouncing all other patterns as wrong. But most of us who are Christians avoid anything as extreme as either of these. Unconsciously, therefore, our minds and lives often become a center for the warring influences of upbringing, secular fashion, and the teachings of the Bible. Yet this last phrase, indeed, separates us from those who profess no faith. For we have an absolute standard of what is moral and right in family life. We do not need to rely on taste, intuition, upbringing, or fashion. Nor do we need to follow the common practice of the humanistically minded mass media and simply *assume* as though self-evident some basic value judgments which are never questioned or made explicit. For we, unlike the secular world, believe that properly human family relationships are those which follow the pattern laid down by God, the Creator of humanity. We follow the design actually revealed to us by God.

Paul says, "All scripture is inspired by God and profitable for teaching, for reproof, for correction, and for training in righteousness, that the man of God may be complete, equipped for every good work."[2] It is by the standards in Scripture that we, as Christians, should form our ideas and test our own life-styles. Within the framework laid down in God's revelation there may be much room for differences of culture, and within these wide limits we must tolerate any cultural differences within the worldwide church. But this basic framework for being "truly human" needs to be studied very carefully. It is all too easy to read into scriptural passages things about family relationships which are simply not there. In this way, it is easy to fool ourselves into thinking that our own cultural prejudices or ideas are God's standards for all true Christians. No one, indeed, can be sure that he is free from this problem. The present book, which is a close study of biblical teaching on family relationships, may well share the fault. But it has been written in a deliberate attempt to avoid it, checking and rechecking to try to avoid reading into the text rather than letting it speak to us.

This book, then, attempts an unprejudiced study of scriptural teaching on family relationships. But there are two things which it does not attempt. It does not claim to be a comprehensive legislation giving specific instructions for solving every variation of family problem. Human situations are too complex and varied for this; in fact, the Bible itself does not attempt it. Rather, the book gives broad guidelines within which pastoral counseling (under the Holy Spirit's guidance) is needed for individual problems. Neither does the present work attempt to present masses of case histories in the hopes that one or other may strike a chord and answer someone's need. This is a valuable thing to do, but there are other books which already do it well. What we are attempting is something which is, in a sense, more basic. It is to give the basic framework of biblical teaching, within which all cultural and personal variations in behavior are equally acceptable in God's sight. Properly speaking, it is only within such a framework that the experience and case-history approach should illustrate for us the human possibilities.

In following such a study, it is essential to have clear in our minds the proper approach to Scripture. We take the Old Testament as authoritative because of the witness of the Spirit to our hearts, and because of Jesus' own attitude toward it. When it says that God spoke to someone, we believe he did. But we must remember two things. First: many of the actions of its characters are reported without comment, God expressing neither approval nor disapproval. Great care, then, must be taken in drawing any conclusions about these. Take, for example, polygamy. It was practiced by Abraham,[3] by Jacob,[4] by Samuel's father Elkanah,[5] by King David,[6] and many others. It was a part of the universally accepted culture of the times, and God never actually forbade it. But silence did not mean consent, and it is noteworthy that nowhere is God said to have commanded a bigamous union. From Jesus' teaching we see that polygamy is inconsistent with God's plan in Genesis.[7] God is a realist. His education of his people into standards of right and wrong was gradual; he concentrated first on the more important points, and did not expect too much at one time.

This brings us to a second point. Most of God's pronouncements were made to specific individuals at particular times. We must take great care in extending the implications of those commands to ourselves today. We see, for example, that Abraham was told to get a divorce,[8] Joshua to slaughter a city,[9] and Hosea to marry a promiscuous woman.[10] None of these are for us to copy!

But, granted that we wish neither to copy patterns laid down for others, nor to write them off as irrelevant, is there a third alternative? Yes, there is. We need to begin with a thorough understanding of the situation and context in which God spoke. In nearly every instance, advice is given within existing social constraints. The exception to this is the account in Genesis 1—3 of God's original intentions for man. The revelation of this, obviously, was made with no social constraints (other than the limits of our understanding). For this reason, the account is of paramount importance to our understanding of God's purposes in human relationships, and the present work relies heavily on it.

But in nearly every other instance, God's instructions are given with particular conditions in mind. When we have understood these, we need to try to discern some of the *motivation* for particular divine commandments. We need to try to relate them to God's unchanging ideal. This may, admittedly, not always be easy to do. Nevertheless, such an abstraction (if it can be called this) is necessary. Then, having made this abstraction, we may try with God's guidance to reapply the principles to our own society and culture.

A good illustration of all these principles is seen in

Jesus' view of Old Testament divorce law. When asked about this, what did Jesus say? First, he went back to the account in Genesis 1—3, which is the only statement of God's ideal for man outside of particular cultural contexts.[11] Second, he understood the particular context in which God spoke (i.e., in a society with many willful and unloving people).[12] Third, he discerned God's motives (i.e., to *allow* divorce as the lesser "evil" in such a society).[13] From all this he obtained an implied abstraction of God's principles (that marriage is ideally permanent, but divorce necessary in an imperfect world where sometimes things go very wrong in a marriage). Thus, finally he could reapply these principles in his own day (that divorce, *whether sought by man or woman,* was a serious step, not lightly to be undertaken).[14]

This is the kind of approach we have tried to take in this book.

CHAPTER ONE

On Being Human

Readings: Genesis 1:1, 26-31; 2:18-25; 3:15, 16
John 1:1-14

"In the beginning God..." So reads the majestic opening of the record of God's dealings with us. In the eternity before our material world was made, there was a personal God. What do we mean by *personal*? The term, in a sense, is undefinable. Each of us experiences a material world (which we describe in physical terms of weight, length, atoms, etc.), and each of us experiences a personal or spiritual world (which we describe in the nonphysical terms of love, hate, desire, right and wrong, etc.). Both realms are real (though, inevitably, there have been those who denied one or the other) and are connected together in ourselves. Yet they are on different levels, and the two kinds of ideas should not be mixed. What we mean by *person* cannot be defined in terms of the ideas and language of the material world, nor can it be described in terms of science (for these relate to the material world). The meaning of *person* relates to the personal or spiritual world, and it must simply be experienced *directly* as we become aware of our own self-consciousness and relate to other persons.

But the Bible does give some further guidance about what it means to be a person, as John sheds the richer New Covenant light on those first words of Genesis. He expands and parallels them thus: "In the beginning was the Word, and the Word was with God, and the Word was God. He was with God in the beginning. Through him all things were made.... The Word became flesh and lived for a while among us."[1] There is, then, an eternal "Word" or "Self-expression" of God the Father, and that Word became incarnate in Jesus. He was not created, but is the means of all creation. He is distinct from God the Father, though sharing the Godhead, and is in an eternal relationship with the Father. Before any creation, only the personal God existed; but an important aspect of that personhood was that God was a *social* being. It is not possible to be a person, in the true sense, on one's own. To be a person means to relate to other persons.

What kind of relationship existed between the persons of the Trinity? We can understand something of this in seeing the relationship between God the Father and the Word made flesh in Jesus. What we there see is that each magnifies the other.[2] Jesus voluntarily follows his Father's direction, even to the extent of making the Father his "God."[3] But the Father seeks to glorify the Son,[4] and proclaims him "God" on his throne.[5] The Son has all things subjected to him by the Father, but in turn subjects himself to the Father—only to find that they are sharing the same throne anyway![6] This mutual self-giving is part of the essence of God who *is* love, and its result is a creative dynamism so that God is all and in all.[7]

Genesis 1 indicates that this personal God created

our world. All the persons of the Trinity were involved. The phrase, "And God said . . ." indicates that God's creation was done through a word, which the New Testament identifies as *the* Word which became flesh in Jesus.[8] During creation, the Spirit brooded over the face of the waters, from which life would be brought forth.[9] The social nature of the person of God is reflected in this, and was extended when God said, "Let *us* make man in *our* image, after *our* likeness."[10] It was a joint decision arising out of the relationship of the Trinity, and the created image reflected that relationship: "God created man in his own image, in the image of God he created him; male and female he created them."[11] As though to emphasize that being personal implies being social in nature, God built in the most basic social relationship (the family) as an undeniable feature of humankind.

In any relationship there must be communication. A basic feature of the personal relationship, according to Genesis, is the use of speech in communication. The first thing God does in either account of the creation of man is to speak to him. The content, moreover, of God's first speech to man is a moral command, showing that the communication concerns such concepts as right and wrong.[12] The second thing God does is to encourage man to begin to use his own powers of using words.[13] To these words Adam associated concepts, consciously recognizing in his naming of Eve the difference in unity which makes up the marriage relationship for man.[14]

The central point here is that we are *designed*. Men are not the result of any accidental development. God made us in his image, intending us to share relationships like those found within the Godhead. When, therefore, we speak of right or wrong actions or relationships, we mean those which do or do not conform to this design. There is, of course, much freedom left by God to man. God did not wish Adam to be a blind puppet. He wished him to be a person able to create and make decisions in his own right—though within a general framework of God's design for man.

Genesis graphically portrays this by showing God as offering all the trees of the garden *except one* for Adam's choice. A tremendous range of activities were open to him to choose, so long as he stayed within the framework of self-sacrificing love relationships which reflect God's nature. Yet man sinned and marred that image of God in him, with immediate consequences in those relationships. These consequences began with his family life, as the man and woman ceased to be open with one another;[15] they ceased to be open with God;[16] and they later found jealousy among their children.[17] The fall brought a need for redemption of a marred creation and marred relationships—a redemption found only in Christ.[18]

It is worth here exploring a little more what God says about the effects of the fall. To each of the three involved, God gives notice of his own judicial action and also of further consequences. God's words to the woman and man imply that, in particular, the fall will make much more difficult their two God-given tasks of "replenishing" and "subduing" the earth.[19] Let us look at God's pronouncements in reverse order.

To the man he says, "Because you have hearkened to the voice of your wife . . . (and disobeyed me) . . . cursed is the ground on your account, in painful labor you shall eat of it. . . ."[20] We should note several things about this. First, God does not say that man should *never* hearken to his wife. Sometimes it is right to,[21] but this does not remove man's own responsibility. Second, this is not an instruction to Adam, but a prophecy. If we took God's words as an instruction to Adam, it would be wrong to use farming aids! None of God's words to Adam, Eve, or the serpent are instructions; they are judgment and prophecy. Third, the Lord deals in generalities. Obviously, not *all* men labor hard; but the point is that in general the task of "subduing" the earth is made a very painful labor. The Lord knew that (historically) the woman's involvement with childbearing would leave the man with the brunt of this work. This is why (we suppose) this comment was addressed to him, although no ban was given on women working in agriculture.[22]

God's words to the woman are: "I will greatly multiply your painful labor and your groanings.[23] In painful labor you will bring forth children and your desire will be for your husband, and he will rule over you."[24] In terms of labor and time, the woman has the major part in childbearing and nursing. This aspect of family—the "replenishing" part of their task—will also be "painful labor."[25] There are also consequences of the fall in husband-wife relationships. It would be quite wrong to take God's words here as an instruction about husband-wife roles. The Lord is not instructing, but pronouncing judgment and warning. What does it mean? The word "desire"[26] means neither subjection nor (as some have said) insatiable lust. Its precise meaning is, however, debatable. One possible interpretation is that in the painful labor of childbirth and nurture the woman naturally turns to her husband. Yet instead of being a loving support, he "rules over her" like a despotic king.[27] Speaking prophetically and (again) in generalities, this has been true.

A slightly different interpretation might be made if we note the great similarity of the language here and in Genesis 4:7: "Sin lies at the door; its desire is for you, but you shall rule over it." Sin's way is to manipulate us, making us think that we are in control of it when really it is possessing us. Cain is told here to master and dominate it. If this were the meaning of God's prophecy to Eve, then it would have very often proven true. Women have often wanted to have a manipulating possession of their husbands, and men to have a dominating mastery of their wives. This may bear some resemblance to what seems to have been God's plan for love and headship in marriage.[28] But it is a perversion of it, a marred image.

The other divine pronouncement, that to Satan, contains a germ of hope. God says, "I will put enmity between you and the woman, and between your seed and her seed; he shall crush you on the head, and you shall crush him on the heel."[29] Through the woman, Satan's evil designs for humanity scored their first success, but through her "seed" he and his designs would be crushed. This prophetically refers to Christ.[30] Her seed (Christ) would confront Satan's brood,[31] but the final showdown would be between Satan and Christ himself.[32] The bearing of *"the* seed," or *"the* childbearing,"[33] was a contribution made by woman alone. This offers her (and us) the redemption of Jesus in the new humanity.

Christ was the second Adam crushing Satan's head. But this second Adam is also collective—redeemed man restoring the full image of God in mankind.[34] The collective body of Christ would share in the crushing of Satan underfoot.[35] But its task would also involve restoring other parts of God's design. This means restoring an open relationship with God himself (through Christ). It means recognizing again the essentially *social* nature of man, in the family of the church. It means restoring in the new humanity the self-sacrificing love which exists in the Trinity, the living of others as oneself.[36] All these are restorations of the marred image of God in man. They will not be complete before Jesus comes again, but the New Testament makes it clear that we need to get to work on them now. And one of the most central aspects of this is the relationship between husband and wife. We have touched on the way in which the complete human unit of male-female in marriage was meant to reflect the Trinity. That love-unity was marred by the fall, but Christians seek by grace to restore something of that true image in their marriages.

We have so far concentrated on the social aspects of being human, for this is primary both to our theme and to Genesis. But what makes up a human individual? Our bodies, according to Genesis, are made of ordinary chemicals.[37] But man, like other animals, was given the "breath of life"[38] and became a living soul.[39] The word "soul" simply means "being." The Bible does not say that man *has* a soul. Rather, man *is* an embodied soul or being, and that being is in the image of a personal God.

Our discussion, at this point, still leaves unmentioned the "spiritual" side of the human individual. Man's spirit is the aspect of him (i.e., of his true self or inner consciousness) which relates to God. As a result of sin,[40] our spiritual nature remains dead unless regenerated through God's Spirit. The physical is born of flesh (including body and soul or being), but the spiritual is born of Spirit.[41] The power for this regeneration is, of course, through the work of Jesus in death and resurrection. Thus, it is written that the first man became a living being, but the Man Jesus became a life-giving spirit.[42]

The Christian's life, then, is on three levels: physical (relating to his body); humanly personal (relating to the soulish side of his being); and spiritual (relating to the spiritual side of his being—i.e., relationship to God). The Bible never gives any reason for man to be ashamed of being embodied. Allusions to "the flesh" often emphasize our human frailty, and that we should not let ourselves be ruled by bodily impulse.[43] The body, if given back to God,[44] is holy and pure, and its natural functions were part of his design. It is important only that we control it and not let it rule us. But, as the Christian knows, we ourselves should be led and directed through the Spirit.[45] The Christian, then, should always be aware of the spiritual dimension; he sets his mind on the things of the spirit.[46] To set spirit over soul over body is to be human as God intended.

Becoming a Christian is an individual thing; yet it has immediate implications for all human relationships. Henceforth no one is to be regarded on only a human level, but as a divine creation made in God's image.[47] The close relationships between husband, wife, and children are now seen in this light, and the mutual responsibilities under God's declared ordering are now recognized. General social relationships change, and in particular God adds the new believer to the church in a close union of spirit.[48] All this is to become truly human; for it is the spiritual person who is normal, not the unspiritual.

To be truly human, then, is to be what God intended. It means being spiritual man, born anew by God's Spirit and attuned to spiritual realities. It means being social man, reflecting the love of the Trinity in our relationships. It means being family man, reflecting in that most intimate of relationships the unity of the Trinity—one unit in several persons. It means showing ever more clearly the image of God through his redeeming power in our lives.

CHAPTER TWO

The Basis of Marriage

Readings: Genesis 2:18-25
Ephesians 5:21-33

The fundamental starting point in Christian thinking is that God designed us to behave in a particular way, and that a central part of this design was that we should bear the image of God. As remarked in the previous chapter, the image of God in the family was marred when Adam and Eve sinned, and Christian marriage attempts to restore that image. What is the image?

God is a Trinity of Persons, dwelling in a unity of Godhead. Each Person of the Trinity has his own will, and yet each seeks in a love relationship to magnify the other. Thus, each member of the Trinity glorifies the others.[1] When God said, "Let us make man in our own image.... In the image of God he created him; male and female he created them,"[2] he showed that he intended marriage to reflect a similar love-unity of more than one person.

Genesis 2 takes a second look at the creation story, with a particular emphasis on the position of mankind. Man was given a very wide choice of activity in Eden, but one thing God did *not* intend for him was self-sufficiency. God said, "It is not good that the man should be alone; I will make a *helper* fit for him."[3] The word "helper" is most often used of God himself as a "helper" of his servants, and is also used to mean "ally."[4] It never means a servant or an inferior, but speaks of a comradeship of an equal or superior. The phrase "fit for him" ("meet for him," KJV) is literally "corresponding to him." This reemphasizes a comradeship of equals. It was this specifically *human* kind of intimate comradeship which God said it was not good for man to lack. This was in spite of man's capacity to relate to the lower animals, and in spite of his undoubted spiritual capacity to relate to God himself. For all the wide choice of life-styles available to man, he had a definite lack of a particular kind of intimate companionship. He lacked the companionship of two allies, where each is a source of comfort and strength to the other. He lacked a close relationship with one who was as fully in the image of the creative God as himself, and so had creativity, individuality, and ideas on a level with his own.

The next part of the account (though the differing chronology from Genesis 1 shows its writer did not intend it to be taken "strictly literally") shows just how much God wanted to enter a dynamic *relationship* with man as a friend. He wanted man to *invent* names for the animals. He also wanted an awareness of a need for human companionship of a particular kind to spring up within man himself. The account of the way in which God took a rib (or literally "side") to make woman has two allegorical meanings: God took something *from* man's side, to make a companion to be *at* man's side, for this is the kind of companionship man lacked. But having taken a part of man's side,

God "closed up the . . . flesh," leaving man incomplete. Woman was not designed to be a duplicate man, but to complete what is missing in man and to add far more. Man and woman are alike, yet different. Masculinity and femininity coexist in all of us, as they do in God himself. But ideally the femininity should predominate in a woman and the masculinity in a man. Together, in the married unit, the perfect balance can come, as the two mingle into one.

This has further implications. First, concerning the unmarried. To remain unmarried may be best for some people or in some circumstances (see Chapter 12). This was, for example, true of Jesus himself. But there will always in these instances be a loss, a missing of the kind of intimate human companionship which God said it was not good for man to lack. The unmarried or celibate state is not to be exalted for its own sake. Neither, we should note, is a true male identity or true female identity to be found in isolation. The self-sufficient male is not truly male, nor the self-sufficient female truly female. True liberation then, for either sex, means finding an identity in relation to the other.

A second implication is that only the married man-woman couple (the basis of what is now called the "nuclear family") can form a complete and balanced human unit. Any form of polygamy, group marriage, homosexual marriage, etc. cannot do this. The "one flesh" such a unit would form would not be a complete "body," but a monstrosity. Genesis itself goes on to draw out this implication. It is *because* woman and man make a complete unit that the nuclear family is God's norm. It is because a man recognizes that the woman makes up the missing part of him that God expects him to seek a wife. So Genesis says, "Therefore a man leaves his father and mother and cleaves to his wife, and they become one flesh."[5]

What exactly does it mean to "leave and cleave?" The word "leave" is a strong one, meaning a definite abandonment or forsaking. The word "cleave" is the same as that used when the Bible says that Ruth "clung to" Naomi.[6] In that context, it meant not only that Ruth had an emotional attachment to Naomi, but that she determined to make her connection with Naomi stronger than any other and to operate as one social and economic unit with her. Her words to Naomi indicate a total sharing of faith, people, and destiny.[7] This is what is involved in marriage. At the time of marriage, the couple deliberately sets out to make the marriage tie stronger than all other family connections. They commit themselves to live together as one social and economic unit. This "leaving and cleaving" is absolutely essential.

It is better if the "leaving" is physical, setting up a new physical home together. But, more important, it is an emotional and mental "leaving." In a Christian family, a single person's natural close ties are with his parents and family. This may mean that they are his closest confidants. But more fundamentally, it means an identification with the family unit involving a mutual commitment to stick together for better or worse. Close friends may share and confide, but seldom have that kind of commitment. At marriage a person's main emotional orientation and commitment changes to the new marriage partner. This is leaving and cleaving.

But Genesis goes beyond the leaving and cleaving to say, "and the two shall become one flesh." What does this mean? Paul interprets it in two ways. At one level he sees it as sexual intercourse—as when he says that sexual intercourse with a prostitute, in a sense, makes her "one flesh" with her client.[8] But he also sees a deeper meaning. He says, "Husbands should love their wives as their own bodies.... For no man ever hates his own flesh, but nourishes and cherishes it.... For this reason a man shall leave his father and mother and be joined to his wife, and the two shall become one flesh."[9] "One flesh" means that the partners see each other's bodies as extensions of their own. This implies, of course, that socially and economically they must be one unit, in a much more fundamental sense than in any other relationship such as that of Ruth and Naomi or of, say, close "apartment mates." Two parts of one body are unlikely to keep separate financial and social relationships. But seeing each other's bodies as extensions of their own must also mean a total physical intimacy, a lack of embarrassment at each other's nakedness.

This aspect of a totally open relationship is seen in Genesis 2:25: "The man and his wife were both naked, and were not ashamed." The openness was marred at the fall,[10] but it can be restored in Christian marriage. The Christian husband and wife have total physical intimacy. Moreover, the physical also symbolizes an openness on a deeper level of "baring their souls" to each other. They should be sharing thoughts and ideas, ambitions and aims together. They should be telling each other their reactions. Yet we must remember *since* the fall to add that openness means "speaking the truth *in love,*" as Paul says. If that is true in a church situation, how much more so in marriage? Any criticism made should be constructive and accompanied by indications of unqualified love and acceptance. The aim of openness is to build up, to encourage, to help.

The essence of marriage, then, is leaving, cleaving, and oneness of flesh. Marriage is not exalted by being spiritualized; and a marriage which has spiritual unity without the biblically emphasized unity on the physical and social level is not really a marriage at all. Spiritual unity is essential to all Christians who work together—especially in as close an association as marriage—but it does not constitute the essence of marriage as stated in Genesis.

The relationship of marriage is compared in two ways to that between God and his servants. In one analogy, God is seen as a husband and his covenant with Israel as a kind of marriage vow. He longs for the pure love of his spouse, but fickle Israel is continually going astray after illicit loves.[11] Yet he is willing to receive her back even after her unfaithfulness, as a loving husband forgives the wife who repents.[12] The other analogy is contained in the word "helper" used in Genesis 2:18, 20. In the other nineteen instances of its use in the Old Testament, three times it means "ally" and sixteen times it is used of God himself as "helper" of his servants.[13] They look to God to give them (as a wife gives her husband) guidance, help, and comfort.

The husband-wife relationship is compared by Paul to the relationship between Christ and the church. Christ and the church, like the marriage partners, are pictured as one organic whole, but in each case there is a difference of role. Husbands are to head the unit as Christ heads the church. But husbands should, on this basis, be prepared to make themselves servants of their wives as Christ made himself the servant of the church. This is the secret of the kingdom of Heaven. The one with any authority is thereby made the greater servant, yet without losing that authority.[14]

Moreover, the headship of Christ over his church does not mean that he smashes his followers' personal identities. God leaves us a wide choice of creative activity within his plan for us (as he left Adam a wide choice of trees in the garden). Likewise, the headship of the husband should never mean that the wife has no individuality or choice of creative activity. The husband should love the wife as his own body, and so of course will wish her to fully develop her potentiality in her own way. She is his companion and "help" or "ally," not his slave. There will be self-sacrifice, not domination, as the husband loves his wife and she respects him, his leadership, and his concern for her wishes.[15]

The question of the difference between man and woman's roles in marriage will be looked at later. But it is interesting to note here that the New Testament teaching about man's headship is not at all specific in Genesis. At most, it is hinted at in Chapters 2, 3, where Adam seems to be God's first point of contact with the unit. But the emphasis is on the companionship and unity intended, not on the headship of the unit. Perhaps this aspect could only safely be made explicit after Christ's demonstration to us of what headship implied. This we will look at later.

As far as the method of selecting a partner is concerned, the Genesis account is silent. In many countries even today, it is the parents (especially the father of a daughter) who are responsible to choose—even if with the girl's consent. This was the practice in ancient Israel, as also in Greece. It is referred to in Old Testament legislation,[16] and in Paul's advice in a particular situation;[17] but it is neither encouraged nor condemned in Scripture. Our modern Western custom of the couple choosing for themselves also applied to certain groups in the New Testament.[18] But the *principle* of marriage itself evidently does not depend on *how* the partner is selected. A mutual attraction is a good start for a relationship, but is not the basis of a marriage. Romantic love is a wonderful and exciting thing, but is not the foundation of marriage. A feeling of compatibility is a useful asset, but is not the basis of marriage. The basis of marriage is mutual commitment, a deliberate "cleaving together" as one unit. Husbands are *commanded* to love their wives, and wives to love their husbands.[19] This is not a command to have a particular feeling. It is a command to act in a particular way—to forge a relationship of openness and sharing and caring in which the partner is seen as part of oneself. This is even an art which can be taught![20]

The basic truth about marriage is that it is a commitment to work together to sort out any differences in an attitude of mutual love and respect. This is a commitment without reservation; it is not something one can enter into on a trial basis to see if one's feelings change later. There can, of course, be extreme circumstances which cause a change in that commitment (insanity, cruelty, etc.); but this is not merely a question of changing feelings, but something far more drastic. The norm is that marriage is for keeps, and that within the security of a committed caring relationship, romantic love can flourish and feelings can grow. But the romance and feelings depend on the commitment, not the other way around.

CHAPTER THREE

Dating and Choosing a Partner

Readings: 2 Corinthians 6:14-16
  1 Corinthians 13

In Bible times, the choice of a marriage partner was generally the function of the parents. Yet, we should note several things about this. First, it is not in any way a part of the fundamentals of marriage as given in Genesis for this to be so. It is not, therefore, necessarily a desirable method, even if it were possible to copy it for our Western society today. Second, there are clearly many departures from it in the Bible itself. Jacob chose Rachel himself because he fell in love with her.[1] Moses seems to have made a heroic impact on Zipporah (perhaps because she had already had an even more devastating effect on him!) and eventually he married her.[2] Ruth seems to have selected her own second husband, though one may suspect that the Lord had a hand in it! Saul's daughter, the princess Michal, fell in love with the dashing David[3] and was eventually given to him in marriage. Of course, not all the Bible characters who chose their own partners made a wise choice. One thinks of Esau and Samson.[4]

What criteria were used in choosing a partner? One clear criterion is that the one chosen should share the faith of the one choosing. Abraham and Isaac both emphasized this, and Solomon, Samson, and Ahab showed the folly of ignoring it.[5] Paul makes the point in a graphic analogy: "Do not be yoked together with unbelievers. For what do righteousness and wickedness have in common? . . . What does a believer have in common with an unbeliever?"[6] This really is a common-sense command. The picture is of an ass and ox yoked together on a plow. The two animals have so different a gait and movement that such a partnership would lead to chafing and irritation, and so is forbidden in Deuteronomy 22:10. This is what happens in the marriage of a keen Christian to an unbeliever. Their life-style and direction in life are so different that it leads to chafing and irritation. More specifically, one of three things may happen. One is for the keen Christian to live a quite separate life from his partner, which means that the true and deep sharing of life in marriage is missing. The second is for the unbeliever to become a Christian, which can happen, but is rare and cannot be counted on. The third is for the keen Christian to become merely "nominal." For this reason, though Paul makes it clear that if someone becomes a Christian he or she should stay with an *existing* unbelieving partner,[7] the Christian should not *choose* one who does not share his or her faith.

A second point which is clear is that a Christian should seek guidance from God. This was shown in Genesis 24:14 when a wife was sought for Isaac. The Christian is one who has said to God, "Your will be done in my life"; he is God's servant. But we should look carefully at this. God has a general plan for each of our lives, but he does not want puppets. He wants to be our Father, not our puppet-master. A good father has a general view of right and wrong within which he wishes his children to act. A father will gladly give advice to his children if asked, but no good father wants to crush originality and creativity in his children. He wants them to create their own beautiful things. Of course, when they are babies they may have to rely very much on his continual advice. But he hopes that they grow into sons, who talk to him about various matters, but who create for themselves. In fact, he is likely to incorporate into his room decoration, say, some of their paintings which were not originally in his mind at all!

God is a good Father. If we talk to him about *any* little thing, he will be pleased to chat. But he really does not want to decide for us what color wallpaper to choose. We may call ourselves his "slaves,"[8] but he himself calls us his sons,[9] his friends.[10] God's final plan for a new humanity is, of course, unalterable by any human act of will. But part of that plan is that the individuality of those who serve him will be worked into the final "new Jerusalem." Each Christian will show a different facet of Christ. This is like the Temple in the Old Testament. It was David's idea, not God's, yet God worked it into his plan and purpose and accepted the Temple as his own. God did slightly redirect the building of it (asking that it not be built until Solomon's day), but this shows the dynamic of the situation.[11] God wants (incredibly enough) to be a co-worker with us.[12] His plan for our lives is worked out in a two-way relationship.

These are fundamental points about the Christian's relationship with God. But the specific application of these principles to the selection of a life partner must depend on the cultural setting. The great majority of Christians today choose their own life partners. How then should they choose? The basis of marriage is commitment, not compatibility; yet it obviously does make things easier if the couple have interests in common and naturally find pleasure in each other's company. Since we do choose our own partners, the obvious way to decide whether these features exist is by some kind of exploratory friendship or contact. But the *kind* of contact which is proper must depend to some extent on the cultural setting. In many cultures, however, it involves some kind of dating, and it may be useful here to think about this.

When a Christian boy and girl go out together on a date, they should be praying that the Lord will guide them in their forming relationship. But they need not expect a sudden visionary yes or no on whether this might be the right partner for them. One of the ways in which the Lord may guide is for them to begin to see some kind of basis for a bond, or to see a basic divergence of interest which indicates that other better partnerships could be formed. The advice of respected Christian friends or pastors may help, though it should be treated with care. An inner conviction may grow, either that the relationship should continue to develop or that it should stop. Perhaps the Lord will even answer, "Yes, that's fine if you really like each other." But there is a danger in expecting too firm an answer too quickly. Ironically, it is the spiritually immature who need the most definite guidance (as with any sons or daughters); but it is the spiritually immature who would be the most likely to mistake what God is saying if they are looking for something dramatic. Sometimes they think that they have received a yes answer in the first week; but as their relationship develops, it becomes obvious that they are really unsuited. This can lead to heartache, hurt, and perhaps even loss of faith or resentment against God when the thing eventually runs into serious problems.

We cannot limit God, though he may sometimes give quick and definite guidance. The more common pattern, we believe, is that a boy and a girl may begin to go out together and gradually get to know each other better. At each stage as it develops, three things increase. One is their openness with each other mentally. They confide their thoughts to each other more and more. The second is their commitment to each other. The longer mutual confiding increases, the more they feel committed. The third is physical involvement. At some stage, either it should become clear that they love each other and will carry on to the ultimate commitment on all three levels in marriage, or else it will become clear that marriage is not right for them—after which, the sooner it is broken off, the less hurt will come. But there is a delicate balance here. Some kind of physical affection is natural as the other two aspects increase. But if it outstrips the other two, then it can only be harmful and may even prevent *true* closeness from developing. It may also "run away with them" and lead them far deeper into sexual exploration than they intended, leading to guilt and perhaps a feeling of commitment based on the physical rather than a love which is based on personality.

There are, of course, no absolute guidelines on much of this. The situation simply did not arise in any form in Bible times. It is a good idea for a young Christian boy and girl to pray together, and if they cannot obtain peace about their actions they should stop. A further thought should be whether they would mind if the (as yet unknown) person they will one day meet and marry were at that moment doing similar things with someone else. Unfortunately, however, we all tend to underestimate our jealousy over such things. But what is certain is that after marriage, any sign of affection and love will be more precious if it has not been shared with a number of previous girl/boyfriends. It may be difficult to picture this at the time of a hot-blooded early courtship, but countless numbers of married people can testify from firsthand experience that it is so. In this sense, some self-control during the short years of early boy/girl relationships can help to preserve an enhanced view of sex for all the later years of married life. The modern "liberation" in sex may lead to much less enjoyment of sex in the long run.

The above has been on the assumption that it is at least a possibility that the couple might become "serious" about each other. But in certain social groupings (e.g., young teens, or late teens for those going on to college), dating is not seen as a possible preliminary to marriage. It is simply for boy/girl companionship. Some books say that such dating should be confined to going out in groups. We cannot accept this, for it can be useful for boys and girls to get to know each other, and to discover more of the way that the opposite sex thinks. This may be more difficult in a group. There is also the problem that in communities where people choose their own partners and social dating is discouraged, there is likely to be much more pressure on a young couple who *do* date to extend courtship all the way to marriage. We have known young couples who were pressured in this way, when really it would have been better to have broken it off. It is dangerous to start married life feeling trapped into it. Rather than risk this kind of outcome, it may be better to allow social dating even though it may bring its own problems.

The object of such social dating is really for companionship, and perhaps because it is socially normal for that group. There is nothing wrong in this. But the physical side should also then be kept down to a minimum. Certain types of physical contact (e.g., holding hands, linking arms, or the "holy kiss"[13]) are seen in a particular society as symbols of affection rather than as "sexual." Social custom will, of course, dictate the normal contexts for such actions. But their object is not sensual gratification. In our view, the physical contact between "social dates" should be symbolic rather than sensual. There is, of course, a thin dividing line. Any physical contact with an attractive member of the opposite sex is likely to be pleasurable. On the other hand, to the Christian *no* contact (even in marriage) should ever just be for physical gratification without also being a symbol of affection and commitment. Yet it is clear that petting, for example, is often not symbolic of commitment, but is a search for physical gratification, even if mutual. Like casual sex, like pornography, this is treating a person as a sex object. This is wrong.

These are hard words in today's climate, and some readers are bound to conclude that we are prudes or harbor some deep sexual psychosis. But we are simply trying to look beyond what happens to be fashionable in Western society today, to the basic ideas of sexuality as God designed them. All Bible-believing Christians recognize actual fornication as a misuse of sex for wrongful sexual gratification. It is not that sexual enjoyment is wrong, but that God intended it to be fulfilled in the committed relationship of marriage. But we find it hard to see a prolonged kissing and caressing between two sexually attractive young people as anything but another form of sexual gratification, even if it does not lead to intercourse. As far as we can see, God intended such to take place only within a committed relationship—i.e., marriage or betrothal.

The one guiding principle which is clear above all others is that in all friendships and relationships we must be aware that a girl/boyfriend is a *person*, not a "thing." When we become Christians, we should never again see anyone else simply as an object, but as a spiritual being for whom Christ died.[14] Our new orientation is to think of the welfare and happiness of others rather than ourselves.[15] If we are to love others as ourselves, we must imagine ourselves in their place and act accordingly.[16] All these things apply with even greater force in boy/girl relationships. A Christian should be careful (without getting conceited) that the girl/boyfriend is not getting too involved, when the Christian her/himself has no serious intention. A Christian should never exploit another for sensual pleasure, or for the social normality of having a girl/boyfriend, when the other person gains nothing from the relationship. The Christian laws of love must operate here in every respect.

CHAPTER FOUR

Marriage and Wedding

Readings: Genesis 2:18-25
Deuteronomy 22:22-29
John 2:1-10

According to Genesis, the essence of marriage is the decision of a man and woman to leave their parents, to "cleave together," and to become "one flesh." As we have seen, this involves:

(1) a commitment to set up a single social and economic unit;
(2) so close an identification with each other that the other person's body is seen as an extension of one's own;
(3) the development of intimacy, of "knowing" one another, one highlight of which is in regular sexual intercourse.

These three points seem to be the essence of what the Bible means by "marriage." But in most societies there is also a specific wedding ceremony in which the initiation of a marriage is proclaimed. Is this essential to marriage or not?

In today's world this is no academic question. Increasing numbers of couples in our society are living together in a kind of sharing and caring relationship like marriage, but (from some psychological phobia, to be trendy, or just because they never got around to it) they have never gone through a wedding ceremony. What should be our attitude toward such arrangements?

In considering this, we should note that the essence of Christian marriage is the same for all human societies; it is the three points given above. But the wedding ceremony can quite validly be different in different societies. The Bible gives no instructions about wedding ceremonies, but it might be useful to look briefly at what usually happened in Jesus' society. There, the first step was usually for the parents of the bride and groom (though not without their consent) to negotiate a "betrothal."[1] This could be done in three ways:

(1) by a ceremony in which the groom handed the bride a small coin;
(2) by a drawn up betrothal contract;
(3) by the bride and groom beginning to live together.[2]

The first two of these were the usual ones, and the third, though valid, was considered blameworthy. In a normal betrothal, the bride's father would provide a feast, and the groom would give him a betrothal gift. From that time, the couple were considered as bound to each other, and could even be called "man and wife,"[3] though at this time they had neither had intercourse nor lived together. The actual wedding came some time after betrothal, and consisted basically of the bridegroom conducting the bride in a procession from her father's house to his own, at which there would be a feast.[4] A benediction would be said, but the ceremony was primarily legal rather than religious. The focus was not on any kind of magic formula without which a marriage was invalid, but on a dramatic portrayal of the simple act of leaving father and mother and cleaving to a spouse. Thus, when Jesus said, "What God has put together let no man separate,"[5] his emphasis is more likely to have been on the reality of married life than on the ceremony of wedding as creating divinely sanctioned bond. Paul indirectly confirms this by applying Jesus' words to marriages contracted under pagan ceremony;[6] so clearly it was not the *religious* aspect of the ceremony which made it "valid."

This background is useful as we consider the relevance of various Old Testament laws for today. Those laws, of course, were designed for a particular society. Like any society, it contained imperfect people and existed in a less than ideal culture. Jesus himself said that the divorce law was to allow for imperfections in Israel's society.[7] He also indicated that in God's ideal, there should really be no hint of the implied double standard for men and women which had existed.[8] Thus, no one could or should advocate a simple copying of the Old Testament laws into a modern culture. What we should try to do is to understand the principles involved, and how these relate to God's most basic statements of design in Genesis. Then we can try to reapply these principles into our own society and culture.

We find that in Old Testament times, adultery was viewed very seriously and was punishable by death. This was because it implied the breaking of a permanent relationship. The sole exception was in the case of rape, where only the man was punishable.[9] But we find that sexual intercourse between two consenting single people was not seen in the same light. Rather, it was seen as a kind of betrothal (albeit blameworthy). Thus, provided the girl's father agreed, the couple had to go through the formalities of wedding and become man and wife.[10] If marriage was not agreed on, then the man was fined.

The details of these laws relate to that particular society. The necessity of the father's agreement (assuming that any normal father would love and care for his daughter) was for the protection of the girl in a culture where she would be the weaker party. But the principles, though not the details, of these laws can be applied today. Those who commit adultery are breaking God's fundamental design for a marriage to be a unit. Although Jesus could forgive such people,[11] he saw this as a serious sin.[12] Similarly, those indulging in casual sex (fornication) were seen by Jesus as committing serious sin[13] for treating lightly one of God's greatest gifts to us. But those couples who do share a committed, caring relationship, without being legally wed, cannot be seen (if we follow the Bible's guidance) in the same category as adulterers and fornicators. If we follow the Old Testament attitude to unmarried lovers, we see them as having established an unauthorized bond, but their sin is primarily social rather than sexual. Society has a right to know (through an accepted public ceremony or sign) when a new man-woman social unit has been formed. But though some kind of wedding ceremony or registration is important to society (and has benefits to the couple as well), it is not the essence of marriage. The essence is "leaving and cleaving," a mutual commitment to live as one unit. It is possible for a couple to experience something of this without going through any wedding ceremony. It is also possible for a couple to go through a wedding ceremony without ever really making the emotional commitment to each other. Thus, one couple experiences the reality of a marriage relationship without being wedded, while the other becomes wedded without ever experiencing a real marriage relationship. This is the difference between marriage and wedding. Wedding is a public pronouncement; marriage is the reality of a committed relationship which society rightfully expects to be announced through a wedding.

Our understanding, then, of the Bible's teaching is that a couple living together in a committed unit without being wed are committing a social rather than sexual wrong. Does this now mean that it is acceptable to forget all about wedding ceremonies? Certainly not. The wedding ceremony (whatever form it takes) has a number of important functions:

The wedding is (most fundamentally) a declaration to society that the couple are henceforth one economic and social unit. Henceforth, a reference to "my wife" or "my husband" immediately conveys the relationship, something which is quite difficult to do when couples are simply living together. The wedding lets others also know that the two are now committed to each other, and so no longer open to approaches by anyone else.

The wedding also makes it totally clear to the couple themselves that both are making a commitment to a permanent relationship. It is all too easy for any of us to forget the exact content of a privately made promise, but publicly made wedding vows cannot be forgotten or ignored. There can be no misunderstanding between the couple about the nature of their bond.

To the Christian, the ceremony is a declaration to God, and an opportunity for friends to come and pray for the couple concerned. The practice of friends bringing gifts to a wedding helps the couple to set up a home surrounded by practical tokens of caring friends.

The ceremony also secures the various legal rights of the partners, for example to inherit in the event of the other's death. This is another side to the issue of letting society know that the new unit has been formed.

Most of these are positive reasons, and should be approached positively. But even if the couple do not wish to be positive, the Christian believes that society has a right to know of the new unit. This is the implication of the Old Testament law we considered.

With so many positive reasons for wedding, we might well ask why any couple would want to live together without it. In some cases, of course, there may be legal or financial reasons. But often the motivation is more vague. Sometimes it is suggested that living together provides a period of trial marriage. But this is self-contradictory. A marriage is, by definition, a firm decision to be *committed* to the new partner. It is not a kind of feeling which might wear off, but a commitment to learn to love each other in a practical way. One cannot make a trial commitment; one either makes it or one doesn't. The Christian does not regard people as pawns whom fate might make compatible or incompatible, but as responsible beings who can choose together to let love grow.

The "leaving and cleaving" of *Christian* marriage will normally therefore imply:

(1) setting up a new relationship, with emotional commitment stronger than any other;
(2) setting up a new social and economic unit;
(3) having regular sexual intercourse;
(4) making a declaration (in "wedding") to society that this new bond exists.

To a Christian, "getting married" should surely involve all these things in some form or other, whatever culture he lives in. If a couple lack any of the four things when they become Christians, then they should put this right before entering the fellowship of a church. This much seems clear. But what of a couple where one seeks release from the tie? Which of the four things should be regarded as crucial and binding? In our view, there can be no simple "codified" legal answer to this, and the Bible does not give one. It is a matter of moral discernment on individual cases, and any simple rules suggested are in our view misleading. Take, for example, the suggestion that only the wedding ceremony really binds. St. Augustine lived for fourteen years with a faithful mistress, having everything but the legal ceremony. Surely if ever moral responsibility to legalize the tie existed, it did then? It surely cannot have been right for him simply to throw her out, to marry a younger virgin of higher social standing after his much publicized conversion? A moral responsibility can surely exist without the ceremony?

Yet, at the other extreme, we cannot agree with those who say that in every case where sexual intercourse has taken place (or perhaps in every case where the girl is pregnant) the couple are morally bound to marry. If we look to the Old Testament law for guidance, we find that in such circumstances the Lord did *not* command marriage as the only decent alternative, but left it to the discretion of the girl's family.[14] This particular emphasis was related to the customs of the time, and a need (in a culture where women were underprivileged) to protect the weaker party from exploitation. But it does show that sexual intercourse *in itself* did not constitute a morally binding tie. This fact should be recognized, however we reinterpret the rule for our own society. Whatever our views on a case of this kind, we must remember that it begins from a situation already less than ideal. It is a question of discerning what will be the "lesser evil," and to some extent this must be culturally based. In our culture, we choose our partners and often delay marriage for various reasons. Thus, while a couple who have had sex in a casual relationship should be encouraged to *consider* marriage, an unwanted marriage resulting from immoderate social pressure may well create a resentment which makes it a failure. Such situations, therefore, call for careful discernment in pastoral counseling, not a rigid legal ruling.

The last question to consider is one sometimes asked by engaged couples. "Since," they say, "we really are already committed to each other, then surely it is as though we are married, and it is all right to have sex before the wedding ceremony?" In answering this, we must admit that sex in such circumstances is not to be classed with casual sex or adultery. There are, however, good reasons why on two major counts such premarital sex should be avoided. The first is the possible effects on the couple themselves. Even assuming that they are both absolutely clear that they are entering a permanent commitment and so "feel" already married, there may be a lingering feeling in one or other partner that what they are doing is wrong. This can cause suppressed guilt, which can adversely affect their later relationship and even lessen their later sexual enjoyment. They must recognize, moreover, that however much they themselves feel committed, others in our present society will not see engagement as a permanent commitment. This means that if they are open about their sexual activity, this is very likely to bring unnecessary disrepute on the gospel. The alternative choice is for them to keep their actions secret, and so begin their sex life together in concealment and fear instead of the openness and joy which God intended for them. Experience has so often shown that the pleasure of the stolen moments of premarital sex is simply not worth the legacy of nervous guilt which it can leave in the mind.

But there is a second count on which premarital sex should be avoided. This concerns not the individuals, but society and others. If they themselves have indulged in such activity, then they can hardly (without hypocrisy at least) advocate general avoidance of premarital sex. This could, in the short run, influence others into following their lead when it would be much more clearly wrong. Paul says that the law of love in such circumstances means that the Christian should avoid leading others into sin.[15] But their attitude could also, in the longer run, contribute to a changing of standards in society as a whole, so that premarital sex became more common. If it did indeed become general practice for "serious" couples, then there would certainly be many cases of misunderstanding between couples about the permanence of their commitment. This is exactly what the public vows of a wedding ceremony avoid. There will also (human nature being what it is) be many more cases of people being deceived and used by members of the opposite sex who really have no intention of marrying them. The norm of restricting sex to those who are "properly" married is not an arbitrary device of God to prevent people from enjoying themselves. It is a wise provision for fallen human nature, to lessen emotional suffering and increase fulfillment by protecting and directing. Any action which lessens the force of such a wise norm is, in our view, wrong.

Even if the couple themselves are not affected, it is a selfish act in view of its contribution to changing the values of society.

None of this implies any lack of sympathy with young engaged couples today and the pressures which they may face. For two young people very much in love, a long engagement can be a great strain. But if this is the case, then the answer is not premarital sex, but earlier marriage. Paul fully recognized the power of passion, but instead of suggesting surreptitious sex he said, "It is better to marry than to burn."[16] Sometimes the social pressures for a long engagement are very strong, but if it is simply so that the ceremony can be more elaborate or the initial house furnishings can be classier, then Paul's wise advice should be taken. Don't delay; marry quickly.

In summary, it is possible to experience something of the commitment of marriage without going through a wedding ceremony, though there are good reasons for preserving weddings. But it is also possible for a couple to go through a wedding ceremony without really understanding what God intends in marriage. This may be more respectable, but it is hardly any less a violation of God's plan. The norm for the Christian is to have both. We need the ceremony, but we must make sure also of the reality of marriage.

CHAPTER FIVE

The Purpose of Sex

Readings: Genesis 2:18-25
Genesis 18:12; 26:8
Song of Songs 3:4, 5; 7:6-12
1 Corinthians 7:3-5

A quite common view of the church's attitude to sex is that of the sociologist who wrote, "The traditional Christian doctrine has stressed the inherent sinfulness of sexual behavior."[1] This may be a sweeping and rather naive statement, but unfortunately it is not totally without justification. When the church, in the early centuries, began to lose many of its original New Testament teachings, many false ideas about sex were introduced. St. Augustine, for example, taught that the sex act was always shameful, and its sole motive should be to produce children. Both these unbiblical ideas lingered on until recent times. The shame over the sex act is reflected in Victorian prudery, while the overemphasis on procreation may have influenced the priorities implicit in the old marriage service which made marriage, "*First* . . . for the procreation of children . . ."

But we must insist that the Christian view of sex be judged by biblical teaching, not the mistakes of past theologians. God's own stated motives for creating woman (i.e., for creating sexual difference) was for her to be a "helper"[2] or "comrade" to man. She was, therefore, created as a sex partner *first* for mutual help and companionship, to make partnership an essential part of being human. The production of children was a secondary feature of sex, for God saw sexual intercourse as an expression of and part of the oneness of companionship and intimacy of marriage. The very phrase, "Adam knew his wife Eve" shows that sex was seen as a way of knowing more intimately; it was the language of companionship.[3] In English we sometimes speak of sexual intercourse as being "intimate," and this is precisely what it was intended to be.

Sex was intended to be within marriage, and in this context Christian marriage (through grace) is to restore the picture of marriage before the fall. At that time, Adam and Eve were unashamed before each other, and likewise the married couple need have no shame in showing each other their bodies. There is, of course, nothing shameful in the sex act within marriage, for "mariage is honourable in all, and the bed undefiled."[4] The Bible always sees sex within marriage as pure and good. For example, the language of the Song of Solomon is in no way inhibited as the lovers describe and long for each other's bodies. The Song of Solomon is, on one level, an allegory about Christ and his bride, the church. But this makes it all the more remarkable how unashamed the writer is of sexual enjoyment. The girl longs to be in a love position, lying with her lover's left hand under her head while his right hand caresses her.[5] The man longs to lay hold on her breasts as on clusters of ripe grapes.[6] This is in keeping with the advice given in Proverbs to "rejoice in the wife of your youth. . . . May her breasts satisfy you always; may you ever be captivated by her love."[7] This kind of passionate lovemaking is heady, strong; it makes lovers say that they are "sick with love."[8]

Marital sex is not only high, holy, and sacred. It is not just passionate. It is also meant to be fun, for this is a part of companionship. The King James Version captures this rather nicely when it speaks of Isaac "sporting with his wife,"[9] a good rendering of the phrase used. Take sex too seriously and it can become a chore—either a religious duty or else a kind of religion in itself, with all the dreary modern preoccupation with technique rather than relationship. God meant it as a thing of fun, to be shared by two people who love each other.

Sex is to be enjoyed. Paul's advice in 1 Corinthians 7, for example, sees sex as something man and wife want to share because they enjoy it. The context of the passage is not at all concerned with producing children, but with giving each other the mutual pleasure of sex. We see, moreover, that Paul is just as concerned that the man not rob his wife of her enjoyment as that the wife not rob the husband of his.[10] It never seemed to have occurred to him that sex might be something to be enjoyed only or primarily by the man. The Old Testament likewise assumed sex to be pleasurable to both sexes, and the woman in the Song of Songs is as enthusiastic as the man and longs to make love. Those people and cultures who have seen sex as something to be enjoyed by men and borne patiently by women have been taking an unbiblical and unspiritual attitude.

Paul's words in 1 Corinthians 7 have other implications as well. The mutual enjoyment of sexual activity is to be suspended only for special purposes and by mutual agreement. It should never be withheld as a punishment, nor given as a reward; to give sex in return for other benefits would be a form of prostitution within marriage. Sex is a sharing in order to know each other more intimately. It is to be given freely from both sides as a symbol of continuing marriage commitment. It cannot, of course, replace a verbal openness, nor be used to paper over the cracks of an uncommitted relationship. But it can help one say, "I care, I am committed" at times when putting this into words might be difficult. Also, the language of "giving" sex is significant. Those genuinely in love usually experience a desire to give themselves.[11] This is the opposite of lust, which seeks to take gratification at any cost. To truly give conjugal dues, as Paul says, means that one is concerned that the other person's sexual enjoyment be complete. Husbands, as we have seen, should be as anxious about their wives' sexual enjoyment and fulfillment as wives are about husbands'.[12] As for any times of temporary abstinence, these are strictly restricted to short times of special prayer if *both* partners are in full agreement.[13] Other than that, the giving of oneself in the sex act, as in the giving of oneself in the marriage commitment, is a command. It does not depend on feelings, though certainly any normal marriage will find the deepest feelings stirred by it.

The Bible says very little about what is permissible in married lovemaking and what is not. Its only specific prohibition is on intercourse during menstruation. This ban seems intended generally, for it is not given in the context of Israel's ceremonial laws, but rather comes in a list of sins (e.g., incest and homosexual acts) for which the *Canaanites* were censured.[14] It is, however, the only specific piece of biblical guidance on right or wrong in marital love practices. Some general points, though, are clear enough.

Since the wife owns the husband's body and vice versa,[15] there is obviously no cause for shyness or embarrassment. The lovers in the Song of Solomon admire each other's naked bodies. It is also clear that, to them, caressing was a normal part of lovemaking, and there seems to be no reason why such caresses should not extend to the sex organs if both partners enjoy this. Similarly, the Song of Songs seems to imply that the couple enjoys open-mouthed kisses.[16] A question being increasingly asked today is whether it is legitimate to use the mouth to stimulate other parts of the body, in particular the sexual ones. It may come as a surprise to some that in an American survey, 77 percent of Christian ministers and 73 percent of Christian doctors saw nothing wrong in such a practice (known technically as cunnilingus and fellatio).[17] Other Christians have found it unacceptable. Since the Bible itself says nothing about it, it is perhaps best regarded as a matter of personal conscience.[18] But two points need to be made.

First, whatever activity goes on, both partners must have a clear conscience over it, and one should not become impatient with the other's scruples or try to override them. This is both because in the love act selfishness has no place, and because it can often lead to guilt which harms both the sex life and the relationship in general. The second point is that whatever forms of love play are held, the climax God surely intended was when the man's sexual organ enters that of the woman (in a visible symbol of the oneness of flesh), and leaves something of himself there (symbolizing the fact that their intimacy has left permanent marks). Nothing could or should become a substitute for this God-given climax to sexual love.

It may, perhaps, be useful to distinguish "making love" from "having sex." The focus of someone "making love" is the other person; the sex is a beautiful and gratifying expression of that love and commitment in sharing. The focus of a person "having sex" is the sex act itself and the techniques of maximizing physical satisfaction. The Christian is convinced that it is more deeply satisfying to make love rather than merely to have sex. Within the positive commitment of marriage, making love can be a time of fun, enjoyment, and sharing, free from any anxiety about sexual success or failure. This is even true for newly married couples. Practical sexual experience before marriage may give better technique, but at the expense of devaluing sex and perhaps also leaving a legacy of guilt and mistrust. It is a far greater thrill for the newly married couple to explore lovemaking together, with their focus on each other as they do.

Yet, though we should recognize all this, there is no reason to value ignorance for its own sake. Lovemaking was meant to be mutually physically satisfying, and married lovers owe it to themselves and to their partners to learn the basic facts about the working of their bodies in this respect. Courting couples should know something of this, to avoid unnecessary temptation of their courting partner. But a full knowledge may best be obtained in the few weeks immediately prior to the wedding. It is not something which will "just come" afterwards, nor can it be gained by reading the Bible and praying. The Bible is not a sex manual any more than a cookery book, but there are adequate other books which cover both![19] A few hours' reading on the basic facts can avoid years of unintentionally defrauding a partner of proper physical satisfaction.

THE PURPOSE OF SEX

We turn now to contraception. Theological arguments have been raised against contraception from three distinct viewpoints:

(1) Sex is just for producing children, and should occur only when the couple actively wants a child;
(2) everyone should have as many children as possible;
(3) couples should exercise self-control outside the "safe period," rather than use mechanical means of contraception.

The first of these is clearly wrong, as we have already shown. The primary reason for sex was for companionship, and Paul's instructions assume that mutual pleasure is the motivation, not a desire for children. In this we believe the exact opposite from Augustine. We believe that to enjoy and share sex together without wanting to conceive can be natural and right, while to use sex to conceive, with no sense of love, sharing, or enjoyment of God's beautiful gift of sex, could be said to be obscene.

We must, however, look at the reasons given for the other two views. One argument used is: "God commanded man to be fruitful and multiply and fill the earth, and this command has never been canceled." This, of course, is an argument for view (2), but not view (3). Its use is unconvincing. For one thing, if we really took it to mean, "have as many children as possible," very very few Christians must have obeyed it, for it would be physically possible for most couples to have at least a dozen children. For another thing, God simply told man to fill the earth, not to overflow it, and mankind already does fill it. What we need now is not more people, but more desire to subdue the earth properly.

A second argument suggested is that contraception "shows a lack of trust in God." This objection would, of course, if valid, apply to any form of contraception, including the use of the "safe period." But is it valid? The Bible never, to our knowledge, forbids taking reasonable precautions against undesirable consequences. Paul, for example, very sensibly tells Timothy to drink a little wine for his health's sake,[20] without any feeling that this might imply a lack of trust. To take *unnecessary* risks would not be trusting God, but would be "putting the Lord your God to the test" in a way we should avoid.[21] It is like any modern medical knowledge. In a situation where medical facilities are not available, a prayer for a miracle may be the natural recourse. But where medicine *is* available, its use should go with the prayer. Our attitude to contraceptives should be similar.

A third argument sometimes used is that contraception is "unnatural" or "interferes with natural processes." But what is meant by this? If "unnatural" is taken to mean the use of human invention, then our whole lives are full of it, from medicine to motor cars. But such human invention is really just a study and use of natural processes for particular ends. When a Christian speaks of an unnatural act, he should not mean the use of human invention, but an act which goes against the *revealed* design of God for man. Is there any proof that contraception (whether the "safe period" or any other method) does this? We know of none whatsoever.

The only Bible passage which has been produced to try to show divine disapproval of contraceptives is the story of Onan.[22] Onan did use the only form of contraception then known (technically termed *coitus interruptus*). But his sin was not contraception as such; it was his deceitful pretense that he was trying to fulfill the social expectancy (later codified in the Mosaic Law)[23] that he should raise up heirs for his dead brother. In actual fact, this story indirectly implies God's acceptance rather than rejection of the contraceptive practice. It shows that this particular method of contraception was well-known to the Hebrews, and yet there is no condemnation of the practice anywhere in Old or New Testament. God, then, saw no reason to state any disapproval of contraception. Thus, while it is possible to argue that the pill, for example, is unhealthy or that the IUD is really abortion rather than contraception, there is surely no reason for any Christian to disapprove of contraception as such.

One last reason sometimes given is not a moral, but an aesthetic one. Some popular Christian writers claim that they enjoy sex more without contraception. This is valid as an expression of personal taste, as long as it is not presented either as an ideal or as a "more spiritual" alternative. If someone feels that the marginal increase in physical sensation compensates for the lingering fear of an unwanted pregnancy, then he is free to say so.

A choice of four alternatives faces the modern couple. The first is to try to have as many children as possible. There seems no particular biblical reason to do this, and probably very few will want to. The second is to have sex only during the "safe period." Not only is this unreliable as a means of avoiding children, but it would seem to go against Paul's command not to deny each other except for a short period of prayer and fasting.[24] The suggestion (sometimes made) that it is a good thing to learn self-control outside the "safe period" is in direct contradiction to Paul's approach. The third alternative is to have regular sex, as Paul commands, but to trust in God that no pregnancy will come unless wanted. This seems to us to be an unnecessary "putting of God to the test," and in practice can often lead to nervousness and tension during what should be the most relaxed and enjoyable time together. The fourth alternative is to accept contraception as a valuable gift of God (like medicine), to be used to help fulfill God's will that the sharing of sex be a flourishing part of a relaxed, ongoing love relationship.

We have, of course, been speaking of sexual love within marriage. Sex outside the committed relationship of marriage is uniformly condemned in the Bible. The word "fornication" *(porneia)* originally meant sex with a prostitute, but had come to include any prohibited liaison or casual sex.[25] Sex with a prostitute or "pickup" involves no permanent commitment or concern for the long-term welfare of the partner. The motivation is simply gratification, even if a mutual one, and such sex is forbidden throughout Scripture.[26] Paul explains something of why it is wrong by saying that sex with a harlot symbolizes a "one-flesh" unity with her, which is inconsistent with being a part of the dwelling-place on earth of the God of love.[27] The self-gratification of *lust* involved in using a harlot is the opposite of the self-giving of *love* in marriage.

A more specific perversion of sex is that of "adultery" *(moicheia)*.[28] In the Old Testament, this meant a man having sex with a woman who was already committed to another. While (in that society) a man might take a second wife, a woman could not take a second husband. Thus, sex between a man and married woman must, if it were to lead to a permanent relationship, cause the breakdown of an existing marriage. Adultery was, therefore, severely condemned in the Old Testament.[29]

Jesus did not come to judge the world, but to save people.[30] Thus, he did not condemn the adulteress when she owned him as Lord, but recognized the sinful nature of adultery in saying, "Go, and do not *sin again*."[31] Jesus condemned adultery,[32] and precisely because his approach was spiritual rather than legalistic he extended the application of the idea in two ways. First, he recognized that the purpose of any laws given us by God is to produce not merely external conformity, but internal harmony. Thus, even to let one's mind dwell lustfully on the idea of intercourse with a woman was like committing adultery with her in one's heart.[33] Second, he reminded his hearers that God had intended one man and one woman to form one married unit. Jesus' interpretation of this (with its implied rejection of polygamy) meant that a married man was breaking or endangering his marriage union by unfaithfulness, as was a married woman. To Jesus, then, adultery included unfaithfulness by either partner; there was no vestige of a double standard.[34]

Adultery is the breaking of a marriage unity which should not be broken. In that it breaks a married unity reflecting the unity of the Godhead, adultery is blasphemous. In that it destroys or weakens the social unit set up by "leaving and cleaving," adultery is antisocial. In that it so often causes a conflict of loyalties in the children of a family unit, adultery may also be antifamily.

But no misuse of sex should lower it in our minds. It is because it is such a wonderful gift that its misuse is so serious a matter. Sex was meant to be enjoyed. As a regular part of an ongoing, committed marriage relationship, it is one of God's richest gifts to women and men.

CHAPTER SIX

Sex and Purity of Mind

Reading: Philippians 3:17—4:9

Lust, pornography, and masturbation are issues which at one time or another concern most men and not a few women in their desire to be "pure in heart." This chapter tries to look at the moral issues involved, and to think about the line between the acceptable and unacceptable roles of sex in our thought processes. As Christians we look, of course, to Scripture for our knowledge of what is right. Yet on these issues, as many others, we need to take care to avoid reading into Scripture anything which isn't really there.

The issues will be dealt with in two sections.

LUST AND PORNOGRAPHY

Jesus said that whoever looks lustfully at a woman has already committed adultery with her in his heart.[1] To "lust" does not mean simply that one is aware that a woman is beautiful, but that one longs for sex with that woman and perhaps even daydreams about it. Since it is only the opportunity and not the intention which is lacking, Jesus rates this as sin.

The most obvious way to define "pornography" is "a written or pictorial representation which induces lust." From our point of view, it seems of little importance whether it is mass-produced or "art," in films or glossy magazines, "serious" or "commercial." It is the effect which matters. When Jesus spoke of lusting for a (married) woman, he obviously thought in terms of a real woman, not a picture. Visual porn is more abstract than lust for the girl next door. Yet the pictures still treat real people as mere sex objects. Any such dehumanizing exploitation (whether for sexual or economic motives) is unchristian. Written material, however, is a more complex issue. Where it portrays promiscuity in graphic detail, it must surely encourage the reader to fantasize himself (or herself) in similar promiscuous situations. This would be wrong. But some erotic literature might portray marital lovemaking. It would be hard to argue that it was sinful to imagine oneself in a situation of married lovemaking. Admittedly, it might be inadvisable for the unmarried reader to dwell on pleasures at present denied him. Also, *some* erotic literature could leave too high an expectancy in *some* married readers. But some erotic literature might encourage married couples in expressing marital love. In other words, erotic literature need not necessarily be pornographic. The Song of Songs is not pornographic, but it is certainly erotic.

Pornography, especially visual pornography, is a virtually inescapable part of our modern Western environment. Sadly, like so many sins, it tends to destroy the legitimate pleasure which it perverts. The sight of a naked woman was once very erotic to a man, but nudity is now so common that it ceases to be exciting.

A different form of pornography is what the Bible calls "foul talk"[2] or "filthiness, silly talk, levity."[3] Some people (including some television comics) think it sophisticated to make continual sniggering references to sex. In actual fact, it reminds us more of the giggling immaturity of children who have recently found out about sex, but are not old enough to understand the loving marital relationships in which it should be used. Of course, sex can sometimes be funny, but to harp on it in this fashion soon removes it from any context of love and sharing and degrades it to a merely animal act. The Christian knows that some people approach sex on a level of animals, but would rather dwell on things which are positive, pure, and lovely.[4]

MASTURBATION

Deliberate stimulation of one's own sexual organs is not referred to in the Bible in any explicit way. Some have tried to include it in the word "uncleanness," etc.,[5] but this begs the question of whether or not it *is* unclean. Others once tried to read it into a condemnation of Onan's failure to raise seed for his brother,[6] or into "abusers of themselves with mankind."[7] Neither are in any way relevant. The absence of any clear biblical directive seems to have become generally accepted by Christian authors in the last few years. Yet there is a wide divergence of opinion on the issue itself, ranging from total rejection to qualified acceptance in some situations.[8] The question troubles many people and often comes up in counseling; so it will be useful to consider it carefully here.

We might begin by taking a look at the reasons

SEX AND PURITY OF MIND

advanced by those who claim that masturbation is wrong in itself, irrespective of its context or its effects on the person doing it. Some comments can be made on each reason suggested.

"It is unnatural." This argument obviously hinges on the meaning of "unnatural." We will look at the term in more detail in Appendix 1, but basically it implies a departure from God's plan for Nature which he himself regards as unacceptable. Could this apply to masturbation?

God's stated design in Genesis 2 implies that he intended marriage to be the norm for mankind. Ideally, then, all adults would have regular sex in marriage. But we do not live in an ideal world, and it is for God to tell us which alternatives are acceptable as a "least of the evils," and which are unacceptable violations of his design. Homosexual activities, for example, were pronounced wrong and unnatural by Christ's apostle.[9] But on the other hand, the single state is one we all pass through, and Jesus and Paul both imply by word and example that to *remain* single may sometimes be the best option in a less than ideal world.[10]

An unmarried person, however, or an unavoidably separated spouse, cannot follow God's intended norm for regular sex in marriage. So what should he (or she) do? To sublimate the sexual drive (through sports, etc.) is not using sex as God intended. To grit one's teeth and "pray for victory" is not what God intended, for he did not mean sex to be fought against but used in marriage. For a man to rely on nocturnal emissions is not what God intended for sex; he designed it for conscious acts of love in marriage. Masturbation departs from God's intentions for the same reasons.

In a sense, *any* of these alternatives might be called

"unnatural" in that they depart from God's design for sex. It is quite open to an individual to subjectively decide that masturbation seems "more unnatural" than the others. But there is nothing to say so in God's revelation to us. Without such a word from God, there is no objective basis to pronounce anything unnatural. Why, for example, should nocturnal emissions be "more natural" than masturbation because involuntary? In fact, their association with erotic dreams may make some men (after prayer) prefer masturbation so that their thought-life during orgasm can be consciously controlled.

The main point is that God only tells us his ideal for sex. To those unable (either temporarily or permanently) to follow this pattern, he gives no specific guidance on the next best alternative. They should pray it through with God individually, but not legislate for others.

"Paul says that it is better to marry than to burn, which excludes masturbation as an alternative." We must look here at the context of Paul's words. In Corinth, there were literally thousands of prostitutes,[11] and it was a normal and accepted way of life for men to use them. Paul had been attacking this practice,[12] and it is in this context that he says that it is better to marry.[13] The Corinthian converts, used to fornication, would have found masturbation a poor alternative to sexual intercourse. If it were really comparable, then its cheapness would soon put all prostitutes out of business. Paul neither suggests nor condemns masturbation as an aid in resisting fornication; we can attribute this either to disapproval or to unquestioned acceptance. But Paul is concerned not with offering the ex-fornicator a less satisfying sex life, but with offering a more satisfying one through transformed attitudes toward *marital* sex.

"Surely it is just self-gratification of the flesh." Underlying this question there usually lies a misunderstanding of the Christian view of pleasure. The Christian does not say that seeking *pleasure* is wrong, but that seeking *illicit* pleasure is wrong. The mere fact that masturbation is sought because pleasurable does not make it wrong. Lustless masturbation is not necessarily wrongful self-gratification. More about this is given below.

"So many people feel guilty about it, so it must be wrong." We should be careful here (and several current books are not) to distinguish guilt and guilt feelings. If we knowingly break a law of God, we have guilt, independent of feelings. On the other hand, a person can have guilt feelings (e.g., about enjoying marital sex) when there is no guilt at all. So one can have guilt but no guilt feelings and guilt feelings but no guilt. Our consciences depend on our upbringing and are not always reliable guides. The Apostle Paul mentions some who preach abstinence, whose consciences are "seared."[14] We can only be sure that our consciences are in line with our guilt when we compare our actions with God's revealed laws. Since he has said nothing about masturbation, we cannot be sure in this case. Our guilt feelings could reflect our upbringing rather than indicate any real guilt.

The above arguments seem to be the main ones put forward by those who regard masturbation in itself as wrong. They are unconvincing. There is also the silence of Scripture. Of course, there are many specific evils not mentioned in Scripture, but masturbation (especially among adolescent males) is a common practice. It seems odd that so widespread a practice is unmentioned in Scripture if the Lord really feels that a straight condemnation is appropriate.

While, however, it is impossible to substantiate a

straightforward rejection of masturbation, there may well be contexts in which it is clearly wrong, or situations in which its effects are harmful. Situations and contexts vary between individuals, and the final choice must be an individual one. Nevertheless, it is useful to ask some obvious questions.

"Is masturbation associated with lust?" Masturbation can be accompanied by or lead to fantasy about illicit sex with other individuals. Whether this involves real acquaintances or pornography, it is wrong. But someone might have in mind merely an idealized image of man or woman, or be thinking of nothing at all. A fiancé might be consummating his marriage in his heart (to adapt Jesus' phrase), which could hardly be called adulterous. A husband or wife might be thinking lovingly of a spouse unavoidably absent for a time. Masturbation need not always involve illicit lust. It must be for the individual to work out with the Lord whether or not in his situation it does.

"Does masturbation lead to obsession?" Old wives' tales about masturbation leading to mental illness are now discredited. But can it lead to an ever-increasing frequency and obsession with sex? It is hard to see why people suggest that masturbation might do this, but never suggest that marital intercourse might do so. Perhaps masturbation might make some individuals obsessed because it fails to satisfy in any deep way. Possibly it might lead some individuals into fornication in frustration at failing to obtain satisfaction. But we are skeptical about generalizing over this. The male anatomy especially is such that the physical release of orgasm normally causes an ebb in erotic feelings for a time. The sexual urge becomes much less pressing. Regular orgasm (in intercourse or masturbation) may therefore cause *less* obsession with

SEX AND PURITY OF MIND

sex. At the very least we must say that this is an individual thing.

One of the problems with the hard-line antimasturbation approach is that some individuals spend so much time and effort seeking victory in the matter that it looms out of proportion in their lives. Instead of an all-around spiritual development, they become obsessed with this one thing. Instead of increased awareness of problems in their relationships with others, they become introverted. Surely, whatever our feelings about masturbation, it cannot be that important to God since he says nothing about it. Let us encourage young people to become obsessed with loving others, not with gaining victory in an area on which God is silent.

"Does masturbation reduce the tendency to seek expression of sex in marriage?" Some Christian books contain careless generalizations on this. Let us first consider the unmarried person. The sexual urge is certainly one way in which God reminds us that "it is not good for man (or woman) to be alone." Perhaps masturbation might reduce this drive. But so might a lot of other things, many of them suggested by books which condemn masturbation. If it is wrong to reduce the effect of the sexual drive, then to sublimate it in any way must also be wrong. Perhaps what we should do is try to ensure that the unmarried person suffers as much sexual torment as possible! Needless to say, this would be an absurd attitude. For one thing, many single people would very much like to marry, but our haphazard modern method of bringing partners together (unlike that of the Hebrews) has never given them the opportunity. For another thing, both Paul and Jesus imply that there are circumstances where some people would do better to stay single, and they

should not be hustled into marriage by torturing them with sexual drives. In fact, if the sexual drive were really their main motive for marriage, they would probably be better single. Whatever Paul's personal advice to ex-fornicators in the difficult times of Corinth, couples in our society who select and marry partners with only sexual attraction in mind can easily later find their marriage is in trouble. Marriage offers a warmth of sharing and companionship with sex being just one aspect. If this is understood, then both masturbation and sublimation are poor substitutes, and one is skeptical about how far they genuinely discourage marriage. Perhaps it is possible that some severe introverts might find consolation in masturbation for their failure to form real relationships, but condemning them for it is more likely to aggravate than alleviate their real problem in this instance.

The extent to which masturbation discourages the unmarried from seeking proper marital expression of sex may be doubted. But there is a possibility that it could do so for those who are married. Marriage partners were meant to express their love in regular intercourse, and it would be wrong to lessen this through any recourse to masturbation. A couple who have quarreled should not use masturbation instead of making up their differences. If there is an unavoidable absence of a marriage partner (e.g., in prison, hospital, or the armed forces), then it may be another matter. But masturbation should never (in Paul's words) make a couple "defraud one another."

"Could masturbation lead to guilt feelings?" We have distinguished guilt from guilt feelings. It is, however, quite possible that even if a person has considered his or her situation prayerfully and has decided that masturbation is not wrong, he or she will still have

guilt feelings. These are real, and they have to be reckoned with. Human emotions cannot be turned on and off at will. The effects of upbringing cannot be undone overnight. Take an example. A young wife and husband have a deeply satisfying sex life. Then the husband is called into military duty and sent abroad for several months. After prayerful consideration, they might decide that during their period of unnatural separation (in our imperfect world) masturbation would be better than obsessional longing, obsessional struggles for victory, etc. Yet one or other might still find themselves plagued by guilt feelings. These feelings, however unfounded, could themselves so inhibit spiritual life that it would be better to stop. This is a general principle. Similarly, there is nothing wrong with having money, but if possessions inhibit spiritual growth, then it might be better not to have any.

Our conclusions, then, are these. It is impossible to substantiate from the Bible a straightforward rejection of all masturbation. An individual unable (temporarily or permanently) to express sex in marriage as God intended will have to prayerfully consider whether masturbation is an acceptable alternative in his (or her) case. The questions about lust, obsession, and guilt feelings (given above) are ones he should ask himself, but his final decision must be reached in a context of his ongoing dynamic relationship with the Lord. But whatever his decision, the whole issue should not be blown out of proportion. If the Lord did not even feel the matter worthy of a mention in the Bible, then it must be because he has more important things for us to concentrate on in our lives. Our basic aim (to which all rules are aids) is to love God and love others,[15] and the priorities God sets for us will reflect this.

CHAPTER SEVEN

Headship and Subjection in Marriage

Readings: 1 Corinthians 7
Ephesians 5:22, 23

In Chapter 2 we looked at the unity of marriage, and the way in which the partners were to act as "helpers." We also touched on the headship of the man in marriage. In this chapter we will expand on this and will look at the biblical view of the respective roles of husband and wife.

Paul says, "Be subject to one another out of reverence for Christ. Wives, be subject to your husbands, as to the Lord. For the husband is the head of the wife as Christ is the head of the church, his body, and is himself its Savior. As the church is subject to Christ, so let wives also be subject in everything to their husbands."[1]

In the Christian family, the husband is appointed to headship and the wife to subjection. Yet much misunderstanding of this has arisen among both Christians and non-Christians. Let us look carefully at the language used.

First, the husband's headship. The Greek word

"head" *(kephale)* does not mean ruler. It is a word used for the top of a pillar, the mouth of a river, the prow of a ship, or the head of a body.[2] In other words, it is not above and separate from, but is rather a unity with that over which it is head. The Bible, in adopting this word, therefore implies the kind of unity which a body and head share. It is an "authority-in-union." Unlike a mere ruler, a head is an integral unit with the body over which it has authority; it identifies with that body so that if one part suffers, all suffer together.[3]

Scripture speaks of three headships, implying three unions. The Father is the head of the divine union of the Trinity; Christ is the head of the "one-body" union of the church; the husband is the head of the "one-flesh" union of the marriage.[4] Moreover, headship speaks of a preeminence over an equality of kind. Thus, in the Trinity Christ could rightly claim equality with the Father.[5] In the church, Christ is the firstborn of many brothers[6] and is not ashamed to call them such.[7] In marriage, the husband and wife are "allies" or "helpers," for she is a "help corresponding to him."[8] Headship need imply no superiority, and (unlike rulership) it does imply union.

Now we should note that it is only in common secular usage that man is called the "head of the house." The Bible itself never uses the word "head" in this way, but speaks only of the man as the head of the wife. The implied picture of sharing one body applies only to the husband-wife relationship, not to the looser ties of household.

Elsewhere, the husband is said to "preside over" *(prohistemi)*[9] his household, but the word used there does not mean to "rule" or "govern" in the normal sense. In fact, a stronger word is used of the wife in the same letter of Paul, when she is called the "despot of the household"![10] The precise interplay of these ideas we may consider later. But neither in "headship" nor in "presiding" are there any concepts of absolute rulership.

If we turn now to the wife's side of the arrangement, the word for "subjection" *(hupotasso)* means to "set in order under."[11] Again the reference is not to unthinking obedience to an absolute ruler, but to voluntarily recognizing legal authority. It goes beyond mere obedience. In fact, the Bible tells children to obey their parents,[12] but has no explicit command for wives to obey their husbands. The nearest it comes is when Sarah's obedience to Abraham, calling him "lord," is given as an example (presumably in terms of her own culture) of Old Testament subjection.[13] But this is an indirect reference, and in any case Sarah clearly had ideas and initiative of her own and is far from the classic picture of a downtrodden wife capable only of unthinking obedience.

Not only is the language used not that of dictatorship-servility, but the headship-subjection idea itself becomes explicit only in the New Testament. There could, perhaps, be an *implied* headship in God's prefall treatment of Adam and Eve. But between the fall and the coming of Jesus, wives are nowhere told to obey or even be subject to their husbands. Perhaps this shows that the meaning of headship-subjection is not conveyed by simple terms like "obey," and that it became humanly comprehensible only after Jesus himself gave us an example of headship *and* subjection in his own life and work. It is in failing to look at Jesus' example that the unspiritual have mistaken headship-subjection for dictatorship-servility. Let us study and follow our Lord.

What, then, would be the meaning of headship-subjection in a spiritually mature Christian marriage?

If we consider first the husband's function of headship, we find Paul deliberately comparing this to Christ's headship of the church. Some Christians have taken this to mean that the husband is somehow spiritually head of the wife; some speak of the husband as a kind of priest, based on Christ's high priesthood; and some even suggest that no one should spiritually counsel a woman without her husband's permission. But all this goes against what is indicated elsewhere in the New Covenant. Obviously, the comparison to Christ's headship cannot be valid at *all* points, or the husband would be an object of worship to the wife as well as her high priest!

To rightly understand what Paul means to convey by his parallel, we must look at the aspects in which he himself draws the comparison. In reading Ephesians 5, we find two aspects made very specific. The first is that the headship and authority of Christ meant a self-giving motivated by love.[14] In a sense, the husband's authority makes him his wife's servant. The second is that the use of the imagery of headship implies that the two partners identify so closely with one another that they are as much a single unit as is a human body. In such a unit, any suggestion of gratification of one partner at the expense of the other, or jealousy or rivalry between partners, would be absurd. Bodies do not behave like that. As Paul says, "If one member suffers, all suffer together; if one member is honored, all rejoice together."[15] In a body, each part in its own way may be creative, original, and make a valuable contribution if allowed to develop. No head would try to stop the hands from being creative, or be jealous of them. The head may give overall direction, and it may make the final decision based on the views of other parts (e.g., if the legs say, "We're tired!"). But its aim is the welfare and development of the whole body viewed as a unit. Jesus, as head of the church, wants friends and co-workers, not mindless slaves.[16] Thus, we are sure, he rejoices in the creation of wonderful art and music by his followers, and rejoices when Christians go on to spiritual maturity. This is the kind of picture bound up in the implied authority of the husband's headship.

The view we have of the wife's "subjection" must again be seen in light of the *unity* implied in "headship," which unity (as Paul reminds us) is at the heart of "leaving and cleaving" in God's design for marriage.[17] We have already noted that the word translated "be subject" *(hupotasso)* means to "set in order under," speaking of legal authority rather than absolute lordship. Thus, Christians are to "be subject" to secular authorities and to those appointed to preside over the church.[18] Slaves are to be subject to their legal masters, and children to their parents.[19] At one level, subjection has to do with the Christian's commitment to an orderly society. Authority is to be obeyed not because it is always right (as an authoritarian might believe), but because isolated acts of anarchy (except in the very direst situations) do not lead to either a better community or a better character in the Christian. Those who have recognized positions of authority are responsible to God to fulfill their divinely given functions, and those under them to obey except in genuine matters of conscience.

"Subjection" speaks of orderliness. But there is a deeper level at which subjection is a basic feature of Christian character. Christians are to "be subject" to one another.[20] This certainly does not mean that they are to be uncreative, devoid of ideas of their own, or servile. What it means is that in an atmosphere of sharing, they are to be prepared to forego their own inclination if it is appropriate. Only against a background of this kind of general Christian mentality are wives told to "be subject" to their husbands.[21] Both the general mentality and the particular expression of it in wives' attitude to their husbands' authority may be foreign to the unspiritual mind. But it is Christlike, for he too was subject, to his earthly parents and to his heavenly Father.[22] Just as Christ teaches the husband the meaning of headship, he teaches the wife the meaning of subjection. It cannot mean that he was servile and lacked originality or opinions of his own. Neither should a wife have these characteristics. As a part of the same body with her husband, she will share fully with him her views and understandings.

But if there remains a genuine difference of opinion on some matter which concerns the marriage unit, then where should the final responsibility be for the decision? One cannot have a majority vote with only two people. Should they let the issue drag on as a bone of contention? Should they shout at each other until the weaker gives in? Should they toss a coin? God's way in marriage is for the husband, as head, to be responsible for the decision, and for the wife to "be subject." This does not mean that she pretends that she agrees when she does not. It means that she tries, with a genuine respect for her husband and his decision,[23] to make it work. To be subject in this sense is much more positive than mere obedience, for it is neither a lack of opinion, nor a sniping, tight-lipped outward conformity while inwardly hoping that the decision will prove wrong. To be subject to the head of a body in which one shares implies an identification with that body, and so with its decisions. This, in a context of love and sharing, is a positive recipe for harmony in marriage.

Now we may ask whether this kind of view of headship-subjection could be called sexist or prejudiced. We should note first that the Bible *nowhere* says that God gave headship to the man because he was better fitted for it. There is absolutely nothing in Scripture to suggest that the woman is inferior mentally, spiritually, or psychologically. In many marriages we know very well that she is not. Could anyone seriously suggest that Deborah was inferior to Lappidoth?[24] That Huldah was inferior to Shallum?[25] That Abigail was inferior to Nabal?[26] The last is particularly absurd. Abigail was superior to Nabal in beauty, charm, dignity, temperance, wisdom, initiative, and faith. The idea that all women are by nature inferior is a foolish pagan idea (held, for example, by Plato and Aristotle[27]) and read into the Scriptures by men too influenced by pagan thinking and male chauvinism.

The Bible, as far as we know, makes only one significant generalization about any inherent differences between the sexes. Peter says, "Likewise you husbands, live considerately with your wives, bestowing honor on the woman as the weaker sex, since you are joint heirs of the grace of life."[28] The phrase used here is (literally) "the weaker vessel." The word "vessel" is used here deliberately because it can *only* mean weaker in body in such a context.[29] As a generality this is true. It is illustrated if we compare standards in unisex sports such as tennis or track, where men and women develop through rigorous training to maximum capacity. But it is only as an observed generality that Peter mentions it in passing. He does not say that *every* husband is physically stronger than his wife. He does not say it is a basic part of God's design. He certainly does not say that because men are physically stronger, they should rule. In actual fact, his point is almost the opposite. He says that in things that matter, women are coequal heirs with men, and so no one should be misled into giving them less honor just because on average they have less muscle power.

There are, of course, Christians who assert that men are somehow "better fitted" to headship. This could, as a generality, be true, but it would have to be shown from psychological study, for the Bible does not say so. But to suppose that *in every case* the man is better fitted in some natural way for headship is both absurd and misses the point of the way God gives responsibility. He does not guarantee that a person's natural ability is always sufficient for the task. He says, "My grace is sufficient for you."[30] For marriage, God chose a simple, unambiguous pattern of responsibility. While there might be much argument in any marriage over who was better fitted to lead, there is no argument about who is the husband and who the wife! God explicitly appoints the husband to headship, and if he relies on Christ (who is *his* head) then God will make him equal to it. This is not a prejudiced view of men, but a realistic view of God. The Christian marriage should enable full use and development of the potentialities of both man and woman, but at heart it is neither man-directed nor woman-directed, but God-directed.

The man, then, is appointed to headship and the woman to subjection. Yet any sensible husband recognizes that on some or many issues his wife's judgment is more reliable than his own. On such issues, he may take her advice against his own inclination. We have here to recognize the difference between institutional leadership and inspirational leadership. A secretary of state, for example, has the institutional leadership of his department. But it is quite possible that he would habitually follow the advice of a brilliant political adviser. In a sense, the adviser would be the inspirational leader; sometimes the adviser might even be the better man. Yet this never alters the legal headship and responsibility of the secretary, and it is he who will be held responsible for the decision. Similarly, there is nothing wrong in a marriage where the husband often follows his wife's advice and inspirational leadership. But in a Christian marriage he is always regarded as the institutional leader and cannot use the advice as an excuse to escape this responsibility. The wife is, of course, responsible for the advice she gives, but he is responsible for the decision itself.

We remember also that the man is to "preside" *(prohistemi)*. The word used designates a leader rather than a ruler.[31] There is a great difference between a president and a dictator. A dictator simply hands out autocratic instructions. A president is the head of a team which works together, and he needs qualities very different from those of a dictator. A good president is one who can bring out the best from his team members, helping them to reach their full potential in the areas where they can contribute the most. A good president knows when to take advice from a team member with more expertise in a particular area than he has himself. Yet none of this diminishes the president's authority or institutional responsibility of leadership. The man, likewise, should seek to preside well over his family.

Perhaps at this point some husband may ask, "How can I act properly as head when my wife refuses to be subject?" Obviously it will be more difficult, but he has here the example of Christ. When the church refuses to be subject to its head, and refuses the joy of sharing as co-workers with him, Christ does not give up. He does not become bitter, or cease to love and act out his headship as best he can. Husbands, love your wives as Christ loved the church, not expecting perfection.

Then, again, some wife may ask, "How can I be subject when my husband is so unreasonable?" The answer, again, is to be like Christ. Even in wrongful suffering under authority, Christ left us his example.[32] So, wives, "be submissive to your husbands, so that some, though they do not obey the word, may be won without a word by the behavior of their wives."[33] Note Peter's words, "without a word." How difficult it is for a woman to be subject, or to see her husband neglecting church or family (as she sees it), without nagging him. Of course, it is right to gently remind him of his responsibilities and to express her opinion to him. But nagging never won anyone, whereas a loving behavior often wins. A wife is not authorized to disregard her husband's headship in a matter of opinion as to what is the best path. Authority is to be disobeyed only when it presses us to go against an *explicit* commandment of Christ.[34]

Paul encourages both men and women to make the best of their marriages even to unbelievers,[35] though there will be obvious problems and such a union should not be sought.[36] Perhaps, of course, it might come to such a point of cruelty or unreasonableness that the marriage itself would be better dissolved. God himself recognized that we live in an imperfect world.[37] But it will not usually come to this.

In general, then, God appoints the husband to headship and the wife to subjection, in a one-flesh unit of marriage. None of us are perfect (whether Christian or otherwise), and we cannot expect perfection in our partners. We need simply to try to live our *own* lives in a living relationship with God—in the light of his revelation to us of what he wants, and of Jesus' example.

CHAPTER EIGHT

Male and Female in Marriage

Reading: Proverbs 31:10-31

This chapter concerns a different aspect of husband-wife roles within marriage. It basically asks whether there are particular interests, characteristics, or roles which are "masculine" and "feminine." Is it, for example, "unnatural" for a boy to play with dolls or a girl to like football? Would it depart from God's pattern for a father to keep house and look after the children while his wife went out to work?

To begin with, however, we should recognize the three possible sources of male/female roles. First, there are some inherent physical and psychological differences. The actual number are fewer than most people suppose, for most differences in character and outlook are due to conditioning. This is the second aspect: conditioning gives us most of our views of what activities we see as masculine or feminine. The third aspect is that God has revealed to us in Scripture certain differences in roles. Now where this is so, one should not assume that these necessarily correspond with inherent differences. Thus, the headship-subjection roles need not depend on any natural characteristic of men and women, nor on any innate instinct. If God says that this is what he had in mind, then Christian parents will deliberately condition their children to accept it. This is true of all moral issues. Christian parents condition their children not to lie, steal, or murder, though an observation of human behavior would totally fail to demonstrate this as "natural" to humankind! Another word for "conditioning" is "training," and that is exactly what parents are supposed to do for their children. But what Christians should be careful to do is to ensure that they insist only on features taught by Scripture; too often Christian teachers have been dogmatic over aspects of male/female roles which were merely their own ideas.

What does Scripture say about male/female roles? An obvious area to consider is that of parents' roles regarding their children. Paul seems to assume that there should be children in a family, and makes the reasonable assumption that it will be the woman who bears them![1] Physically, only the woman is equipped to breast-feed the baby, and modern evidence seems to show that it is better physically and psychologically for the child to be breast-fed in its early weeks. The baby should relate to both parents, but the mother-child bonding which can be achieved in that most intimate and wonderful of experiences is particularly important. Women's lib supporters, such as Germaine Greer, tend to write off breast-feeding;[2] but if it is seen as important and enriching, then it would seem to point to a greater role for the mother than the father in the nurture of the young baby. Yet, even here we must be careful. Although some Christian books give warnings of dire consequences if fathers become too involved in baby-care, there is nothing in the Bible to limit this to being a "female" activity. In fact, the King James Version speaks of "nursing fathers."[3] The Hebrew word used may mean more a male guardian who (like Eli with Samuel[4]) had the care and responsibility of bringing up a child. But this paternal care could begin even with a babe.[5] Scripture definitely refers to child training as being partly the responsibility of the father.[6] There is, furthermore, no indication that the mother's authority over the child is in any sense a derived authority (as some Christians claim). The child is told to obey both father and mother, and Scripture assumes that the "instruction" or training given by the father is the same as the "law" (KJV) laid down by the mother.[7] There is no evidence at all that looking after the children (apart, obviously, from breast-feeding) is seen as a specifically female role.

What of the question of who goes out to work? Again, some Christians say that man should be the provider, while woman keeps house. What evidence is there that this is God's ruling? Very little. The husband is supposed to "preside over" the household.[8] But a stronger word (literally "despot of the household") is used of both the husband *and* the wife.[9] Paul evidently thinks that whatever is involved in being mistress of a household occupies enough of the woman's energies to prevent her becoming a busybody, but adds little to what is said in Proverbs 31 about the varied nature of her activities. The word translated "despot of the household" was, in fact, the normal Greek term for the master or mistress of a house.[10] But this helps us little since Paul clearly rejected the Greek culture where a wife was a drudge and childbearer while the husband sought pleasure and companionship from other women.[11] Elsewhere Paul suggested teaching young wives to be (among other things) "house-workers" *(oikouros).*[12] But his motive is given in the following phrase, "so that no one will malign the word of God." The whole passage is in the context of the witness to the surrounding people. Where no fundamental inconsistency with the gospel was involved, Paul was all for keeping local custom.[13] But he surely would not have expected that an incidental reference to housework (contained in an instruction to Cretan housewives to have a good witness to the neighbors) would one day be used in an entirely different culture to suggest that women should never leave the household sphere.

The Bible, then, gives little specific instruction about the husband's or wife's roles. It may sometimes be incidentally assumed that women mentioned have certain roles, but it is never stronger than this. It may seem to us a sensible arrangement for a mother with a young baby to look after the home, while father goes out to work. If these roles continue when the child is older, well and good. But the arrangement is based on convenience rather than biblical revelation, for the Bible says nothing about it. A wife who was the main wage-earner would have to be content that her husband, as head, would have the final say on how the money was to be spent; but in the one-flesh love of marriage, this is quite possible. The man's headship does imply that he has the final responsibility to see that the family is provided for. But it is quite possible that the provision could be made through another member of the family (wife or son or daughter), provided of course that the arrangement is a result of love and not selfishness on the part of the husband.

But in all this, the Bible seems no more to condemn a career woman than a career man. In either case, love of God and one's family should take precedence over love for money. Paul's first convert in Europe was Lydia, a businesswoman in her own right, and it was in her house that he first stayed.[14] In Corinth, Paul stayed with his two co-workers Priscilla and Aquila, "because he was of the same trade ... *they were tent-makers.*"[15] Both apparently shared in the employment, as both shared in giving spiritual instruction,[16] and there is no hint that it might be proper only for husbands to work at a trade. This is, after all, in line with the "good wife" of Proverbs 31, who seems to use her own initiative to engage in manufacturing, agriculture, and social work! Later, women seem to have been accepted to participate even in the construction industry.[17]

Yet some Christians have argued that man should be the provider. In doing so, they seem to forget that during Jesus' ministry his *women* followers acted as patronesses and provided for him.[18] Thus, though one might say that the man (as head) has the ultimate responsibility for ensuring that the family *is* provided for, the actual pattern of provision can surely be worked out by the couple in whatever way they agree. God does not specify for them. All that can be said is that a man who truly loves his wife (as Christ loves the church) will wish neither to patronize nor exploit her.

Now with all this background, one is astonished to find the feminist Simone de Beauvoir attributing to Paul the following view:

> Since the husband is the productive worker, he is the one who goes beyond family interest to that of society. Opening up a future for himself through cooperation in the building of the collective future, he incarnates transcendence. Woman is doomed to the continuation of the species and the care of the home—that is to say, to immanence.[19]

MALE AND FEMALE IN MARRIAGE

Paul admittedly assumes as factual (with good evidence to the best of our knowledge) that only women can bear children.[20] But where does he state any of the rest of all this? Nowhere we know of. It was certainly the pagan Greek culture at that time to assume such a pattern. There may have been some Christians in the past who assumed that it was the only pattern approved by God, but we repeat: we know of nothing in Scripture to support it. God's design was for two "allies" or "helpers," but he specified no particular pattern about who should provide which aspect of family need. The curse of the ground directed at Adam was a prophecy, not a prescription for action,[21] and agriculture is not seen as an exclusively male affair.[22]

All of us have been brought up in particular societies, and so see certain roles as male and others as female. If it helps our sense of personal identity to keep to these, well and good. But unless we can support them as a part of God's design revealed in Scripture, we have no right to press them upon others. The Bible does not teach that the man need necessarily be the "spiritual leader" in marriage. It does not insist on his being material provider. It does not give him any more basic claim to children's obedience than his wife. All that it says is that as the head of the "one-flesh" unity of marriage, man is to "preside." The decisions are to be made by the whole unit, but in the event of a continuing difference of opinion, the husband has the chairman's deciding vote. It is his responsibility to determine whether to follow his own or his wife's judgment, and the wife is to be subject to the decision (unless it is contrary to a direct divine commandment).

One further point needs to be made. We do not believe that there is in Scripture any clear revelation about what some Christian writers call "spheres of influence" for husband and wife. We are free to work out our own patterns and areas of responsibility in a dynamic relationship with God. Nevertheless, we believe that any wise husband will recognize that his wife does need to have some areas where she is solely responsible and can exercise her own choice. She, too, may be a child of God whom he is bringing into maturity, which involves making decisions. She too has a need to express individuality as she unfolds her part of the multicolored nature of Christ.[23] A failure to recognize this could leave her feeling crushed and dominated. It is, moreover, a good idea to talk out areas of responsibility (individual and joint) early in (or before) marriage. For one thing, the husband and wife may come from families with different traditions; and different expectancies could lead to conflict. For another, it enables a more conscious and intelligent pattern to be thought through than if it is simply left vague. Needless to say, this cannot be a once for all thing. Areas may change, and differing needs may arise. But within a loving relationship of mutual concern and respect, the partners can continue to develop as "allies" in all senses of the word.

We may now turn to consider a matter already touched on. What differences should there be between male and female attitudes toward sexual rights and enjoyment? What we find is that scriptural teaching on this is very explicit in terms of equality. It must, of course, be recognized that before the completeness of the revelation of God in Jesus, some elements of attitudes in the Old Testament society were less than ideal. Underlying this was their toleration of polygamy. This was common in surrounding cultures, and God did not expressly forbid it. But it was not in line with God's basic design in Genesis, and whenever mentioned in Scripture it seems to lead to family problems of one kind or another.[24] Yet it was tolerated, and with it a lingering double standard. This meant that sex between a married woman and unmarried man was adultery, while sex between a married man and unmarried woman was perhaps not (for he could marry the second woman). Possibly this should be seen as a protection of the rights of women in a cultural context where these were often ignored. But Jesus made it very clear that he regarded sex between a woman and married man as adultery also.[25] This was revolutionary. Paul is but drawing out the implications of this when he makes it clear that casual sex for the man is equally wrong.[26]

Paul, moreover, makes it clear that the husband's and wife's sexual rights are identical. In 1 Corinthians 7 he gives a mixture of authoritative teaching and personal suggestions for application in their circumstances, which is quite revolutionary. Almost every point is repeated from both persons' point of view. Thus, the husband "has his own wife," but equally the wife "has her own husband." The concept of possession goes both ways.[27] "The wife does not rule over her own body, but the husband does." Is this sexism? No, for the next words are, "likewise the husband does not rule over his own body, but the wife does." They both have joint ownership! In verse 5 Paul says, "Do not refuse one another." In other words, have regular sex to satisfy *both* parties. Beginning in verse 12, he says that if one partner is unbelieving, then the other should not leave him/her—whichever it is. The whole passage puts the sexes on exactly equal footing. Even verse 18 should not read, as in the KJV, "Is any man called . . ." but "Is any one called . . ."

One of Paul's main points later in the passage is

that we must not copy others, but find God's will individually for our lives. He gives as his personal opinion that in times of particular difficulty, it may be better to remain single or betrothed.[28] For this reason, in spite of his advocacy of marriage elsewhere,[29] he has sometimes been labeled as antifeminist or even antisex. But his only reason—again we note, given in terms of both the man and the woman—is that in such circumstances it may be an unnecessary tie. This is precisely because in his high view of marriage, the married man is properly "anxious ... to please his wife" and the married woman "anxious ... to please her husband."[30]

How could this be antifeminist? The only hint of any inequality is that the final decision on whether a widow should marry is assumed to rest with herself, but with a virgin the decision rests with her father.[31] Paul simply assumes this (which was practice for both Jews and Greeks), without any comment either way on the desirability of the custom itself. Since, however, he elsewhere instructs fathers not to provoke their children, it can be imagined what advice he would give a father who was intending his daughter's marrying or not marrying against her will.[32] But this concerns selection of partners.

Within marriage, any idea of one-way sexual rights is demonstrably against Paul's explicit teaching. It is also hard to see how some Christian writers apparently get the idea that man's headship means he is to be the initiator in sexual lovemaking. Why should he be? The wife has as many sexual rights over her husband as husband over wife, and should seek them if she feels like exercising them. If ever they do have a short period without lovemaking, it will be during a time of special prayer (when they may also, perhaps, abstain from another good thing, food, in fasting). But this must be by mutual agreement.[33] The husband's headship is *not* sufficient authority to deny his wife her sexual rights unless she agrees. Whatever happened to this revolutionary biblical teaching on sex in the centuries of male chauvinism which followed?

We turn now to a very basic question. It is somewhat abstract and has been left until some of the more concrete issues have been considered. It concerns the distinction between masculinity and femininity as such. In Chapter 2, we looked at the account of God using Adam's "side" to make Eve. Having taken a part of man's side, God "closed up the flesh," leaving man incomplete. This surely was not meant to teach that man is physically lopsided, but that his physical/mental makeup has predominately one side of human nature. We might call this "masculinity." The side of human nature which predominates in woman we might call "femininity." Both are in God, for we were made "in God's own image . . . male and female."[34]

How, then, can we know which characteristics are properly to be regarded as masculine and which feminine? God, unfortunately, nowhere gives us in the Bible any direct description of how *he* sees these. We have to work from clues only.

Perhaps we might begin by asking whether there is a hint to be found in the reference to God himself as "he." This is possible, though it is hard to say exactly what that hint is. Mankind *male and female* were made in God's image; so to call God "he" rather than "she" must be something of a language convention. No one would want to call a personal God "it"; so it had to be either "he" or "she." Since God has given the headship within marriage to the man, and God is himself the source of all authority, it would have seemed odd to pick "she" to describe God. But, of course, the picture of God as our Father does not exclude the use of a motherhood picture as well.[35] If, then, we glean anything from this, it is a notion of strength and authority as masculine, and tenderness as feminine. God has both equally. But the link is slight.

Can we, then, discover clues in innate or inborn characteristics of men and women? Has God, in other words, laid them down in the way he *made* men and women? There may, indeed, be such inborn characteristics, but it is difficult to discover them. Modern study comparing different societies and cultures has shown that much of what we see as masculine or feminine is affected by social conditioning.[36] Thus, a girl acquires or exaggerates those characteristics in herself which she is told are feminine, and a boy those which he is told are masculine. The power of this conditioning appears to be very strong compared with any inborn influences. Since it is, of course, impossible to find anyone in whom the inborn characteristics have *not* been affected by some form of conditioning, this makes the inborn very difficult to detect. All that one could make is a kind of statistical argument: whenever social conditioning starts to develop a particular characteristic as masculine, it is *more likely* to take and exaggerate or modify an inborn characteristic of men than one of women. Thus, looking at the world as a whole we should expect a majority of societies to have their social conditioning in line with the faint inborn characteristics. This is a dangerous line of argument in a fallen world; but if we follow it, then undoubtedly the majority of world cultures have seen masculinity as implying strength or even aggressiveness, and femininity as tenderness or even softness.

This may also relate to another possible clue, the

purely physical differences. We noted that, as Peter said, the man has on average greater muscle power than the woman, while softness is the special quality of the woman in her bodily design for suckling tiny babies. Here again, strength and tenderness are twin ideas.

The roots of the Hebrew words for male and female, man and woman, if anything confirm this. The roots of the words in Genesis 1:27 are obscure, but seem to relate purely to the physical appearance of the distinctive male and female organs. The words used in Genesis 2:18-23 seem, however, to be from roots denoting "the strong one" and "the delicate one."[37] This confirms our previous ideas.

Now this suggestion of strength for masculinity and tenderness for femininity should be treated with care. Our own Western cultures seem in the past to have carried this much too far, and we do not want men and women to become caricatures. In the Song of Songs, for example, there do seem to be slightly more hints of strength for the man and softness for the girl; yet the girl also uses words like "sweetness" to describe her man. Jesus, moreover, did not try to keep a stiff upper lip in public, but wept openly.[38] We should beware lest our social conditioning make us caricature the masculinity or femininity proper to men or women. It is a sobering thought that Satan's parodies of Christ and the bride in Revelation are the beast and the harlot, hideous caricatures of masculinity and femininity.[39]

Two last points should be made. One is that it is entirely possible that (within very general frameworks) God intends humankind to create something of their *own* masculinity and femininity. This could, indeed, be a part of the creativity within the Christian's dynamic relationship to God, to show God's "manifold wisdom" in the new humanity of Christ.[40] It is true that "in Christ there is no male nor female,"[41] but in the context Paul is surely speaking of a lack of any spiritual class distinction. He does not mean that the enriching individual differences are to be wiped out in grey monotony. Neither, in our view, should Jesus' teaching that marriage is transcended in Heaven[42] imply that masculinity and femininity as such will be abolished.

The other point is that one should beware of the practical implications for someone in a particular society. Although much of what is seen as masculine or feminine in a society may be convention, this does not mean that a Christian can behave in any way he feels like. Take the question of clothing. Very obviously (see also Appendix 1) what is seen as men's (or women's) clothing depends on social convention. But we are forbidden to dress in clothing which our society views as properly belonging to the opposite sex. This has to do with our *motives*. Likewise with masculinity and femininity. If we deliberately adopt characteristics which we see because of our upbringing as more proper to the opposite sex, then for us this is wrong. Our motive would be a desire to change roles, to act out a role we see as that of the opposite sex. In this context, "whatever does not come from faith is sin."[43] But the individual for whom this is a problem must sort it out for himself through prayer and Christian counseling. It cannot be legislated.

All this may strike the reader as rather vague in comparison with the rest of this book. It is. The Bible is itself vague on the subject. So we aim to do only two things. First, we reaffirm (against some modern liberationists) that it is right and enriching to distinguish between masculine and feminine. Second, we urge care upon our fellow-Christians in making assumptions about what specific characteristics to link with the masculine or feminine ideal.

In summary, there are different roles for husband and wife in marriage, along lines of headship-subjection. Yet we must be careful not to read into these roles more than the Bible indicates. All that we can say is that one should never seek (as, for example, some liberation movements do) to try to define true manhood or womanhood in isolation. The whole true nature of humankind can be seen only in the balance of the married unit in which God designed it.

CHAPTER NINE

Family Relationships

Readings: 1 Corinthians 13:4-7
Ephesians 6:1-4
Hebrews 12:5-11

"Our Father, who art in heaven..." So millions of Christians address God. But what does it mean to have a loving parent-child relationship? Such a relationship must begin with the unconditional love of the parent for the child, as God loved us.[1] The parents' love should not depend on the child's behavior, nor on the (perhaps weak) evidence of his love in return.[2] This love, furthermore, should be continually *expressed,* for we know of love only through its action.[3] This not only applies to physical provision,[4] but emotional; this means a giving of oneself to the child.[5]

In human terms, children (whether boys or girls) all need eye contact, physical contact, and focused attention from birth and throughout childhood.[6] Jesus himself recognized this, and made time to give attention to the children and to make physical contact with them in his blessing.[7] The good parent has time for his child, and is interested in every little thing about that child.[8] He enjoys talking with his child and respects his child as an individual.

Thus, although the father knows his child's needs, he likes the child to express them.[9] He likes to listen to and respond to any reasonable request the child makes.[10] Gifts are not, of course, a substitute for sharing together, and in this way are secondary to it. Yet, the good parent does not seek to foster dependence, but to have the child grow up to be a true "son" (or "daughter") and take up his inheritance.[11] In a good relationship, there will be a genuine pleasure in doing things together, a sharing of enjoyment like the returned prodigal son and his father, rather than a grudging obedience like the elder son in the parable.[12] But again, the parent will respect the creativity and originality in his child and seek to encourage it, just as our creative God encourages creativity in his children, who are made in his image. Each child will be valued individually, as an individual with his own contribution to make. The parent will take him seriously.

Jesus certainly did this with children. For example, he used the offering of a lad with a few loaves and fish.[13] He made time for children, and this in spite of his disciples' evident wish to get on with the "really serious" discussion about divorce, etc.[14] His kingdom, he said, was made up of children and those with childlike qualities, and the welcome we give to children reflects our attitude to Jesus and what he values.[15] Thus, the Pharisees' evident outrage at the children creating a disturbance in God's Holy Temple really reflected their attitude to the message of Jesus and its simplicity.[16]

Jesus rebuked the Pharisees. Yet how often today do we refuse to welcome children (with all their exuberance) into our services, but make them sit in unnatural silence or banish them to the church nursery? How often do we fail to recognize them as members of the kingdom, or treat them less seriously than Jesus himself evidently expected to be treated at the age of twelve?[17]

The good parent will also be proud of his children[18] and will praise their achievements. Yet, he will not make his love or acceptance dependent on this achievement, nor try to live vicariously through them. True parental love is unconditional and unselfish.

True parental love also involves discipline. One of the proverbs quoted in Hebrews is: "For the Lord disciplines him whom he loves, and chastises every son whom he receives."[19] Paul says, "Children, obey your parents in the Lord, for this is right.... Fathers, do not provoke your children to anger, but bring them up in the discipline and instruction of the Lord."[20] Discipline and love go together, but we must be careful about this word "discipline." The Greek word can mean "chastise," but really it has the wider meaning of training and instruction.[21] It is not merely, or even mainly, a question of appropriate punishment schemes. It is not merely a question of "behavior reinforcement" (i.e., rewarding desirable and punishing undesirable behavior). Such emphases might be suitable in animal training, but here we are dealing with a love relationship between personal beings, between parents and child.

The instruction will begin in the attitude of the parent to the child, for from this the child will learn his first lesson. A child learns to respect others' feelings through a genuine respect for personhood, as his own parents respect his individuality—not through behavioral reinforcement. More basically, a child learns the way of love by being loved unconditionally—not through any system of punishment and reward. How strange that some Christian parents who proclaim a gospel of grace try to teach their children love through a system of works! Our discipline should be modeled on that of our Heavenly Father.

We must, of course, recognize that chastisement and reinforcement can both play some part. But we should note that in Greek (and Hebrew), there is no connection between the word "discipline" and the word "punishment."[22] A judicial punishment means that a person receives his just deserts for a misdeed simply because the deed was wrong. It need not imply any motive of correction. It is the rightful function of *government* to administer punishment[23] (although some modern governments reject this idea of justice), but the Bible never uses it in a context of parents and children. It speaks of "discipline," the motive of which is clearly corrective rather than punitive.

This is important because "punishment" relates simply to the deed, whereas "discipline" should be more flexible, varying treatment according to the likely effects. A child who disobeys deserves punishment, but if he already shows *real* repentance, then true discipline might involve immediate acceptance and reassurance rather than chastisement. This would teach the child more truths about forgiveness, whereas otherwise he might be entirely puzzled by the words, "He does not deal with us according to our sins, nor requite us according to our iniquities. . . . As a father pities his children, so the Lord pities those who fear him."[24] This, of course, opens the parent to the possibility of a child saying "sorry" insincerely. It leaves parents with the difficult task of discerning true repentance from mere fear of the consequences.

But unfortunately *no* system of discipline can escape the need for discernment. Law (and punishment) knows only of rules with no exceptions; but discipline deals with the person, not the sin. Thus, while consistency is a good thing, to be totally inflexible in reaction would be to treat a person like a machine, and this can have disastrous consequences. What is important, however, is that any variation in reaction is genuinely based on discernment of the needs of the child, not on the parents' mood.

Yet, biblical love and discipline include physical chastisement where necessary, and Proverbs goes as far as to say: "He who spares the rod hates his son, but he who loves him is careful to discipline him."[25] Here again "the rod" fits into an overall picture of "discipline," within which we see more clearly in New Testament light a role of unconditional love. But the word "rod" in any case implies more than physical force, for it can also mean "sceptre"[26] and is thus a symbol of authority. When it is used to chastise,[27] it therefore symbolizes the wielding of authority, not an arbitrary use of personal violence in frustration. But the rod should also be used to guide and protect like a shepherd's rod.[28] In this connection David said, "Your rod and your staff, they comfort me."[29] It is a comfort to a child to know that an authority exists, both for correction and protection. All children find a need at times to test authority, to find out if deliberate disobedience brings any reaction. To find that it does brings security and comfort. The use of physical chastisement in such a context can be right and can lead to healthy harmony in a home. A smack is a short, sharp assertion of authority. After a short period of crying, it can be followed by immediate expression of acceptance and reassurance. If a child deliberately disobeys, then the other alternatives are:

to ignore it and have the child lose any secure respect for authority; to use a form of punishment which could drag on without any real emotional release; or to have a situation where the parent is continually whining and nagging at the child. None of these three are acceptable.

In suggesting that punishment is appropriate for willful challenge to authority, we are in a sense again following God's dealings with us. A person who persists in known sin will be excluded from fellowship in Heaven and on earth until he repents.[30]

This is important as we answer those "progressives" who ask what right parents have to use force to impose their wills on children. Parents have a God-given authority and responsibility (which no state can take away) to use physical correction in a right discipline of their children. But it is a misrepresentation of this authority to suppose that it involves merely the clash of preferences, with the parent selfishly insisting on his preference when the child's would be equally valid. The parent teaches the child what is *right*—not his own ideas, but God-revealed standards of right and wrong. This forms a framework within which the child should have ample room for self-expression if his parents truly love him. Paul's instructions are most careful of the child's rights. Parents are instructed to bring their children up "in the discipline and instruction of the Lord"—not in the parents' own ideas and preferences. Furthermore, he specifically tells parents not to use their authority wrongly and so provoke their children to anger and frustration.[31] We must treat this instruction with care.

A toddler, for example, may exhibit anger when he is prevented from touching a fire. He may become angry when he is chastised for deliberate rebellion.

But this, surely, is not what Paul means. Rather, it must refer to the deep-seated frustration which burns inside over a long period, the kind of anger he forbade earlier in the letter.[32] An overbearing or unreasonable parent may provoke this kind of anger. An overindulgent parent may also be laying up a later store of anger and frustration as the growing child finds that he cannot get his own way with others as he has learned to expect from his parents. But if rightly used, chastisement does not provoke this kind of anger. After a healthy expression of anger or pain in crying, there is reconciliation and the feeling that love continues. Only ineffectual chastisement leaves lasting anger; there is irritation, but no real emotional release and no reconciliation. Rightly used authority and chastisement lead to harmony, not anger and frustration.

We should further note that God-given authority teaches by example and not only by instructions. Thus, when God gave the fundamental command to "Love the Lord your God with all your heart and with all your soul and with all your strength," he went on: "These commandments . . . are to be upon your hearts. Impress them on your children. Talk about them when you sit at home and when you walk along the road, when you lie down and when you get up. . . ."[33] Your children will best learn the love of God if it is a remembered, experienced, and verbalized reality to you in every activity of your life. The next few verses in the passage symbolically indicate that they should be bound on your hands (what you do), and on your foreheads (what you think), and on your gates (the principles of your home). It will be no use telling your children about God's love if it is not a reality in your own life. The authority of parents, like that of elders,[34] is to lead by example.

Jesus also used this principle in teaching his disciples about authority. To *show* what a leader should do, he washed their feet; he did more than talk about it.[35] Children are to be imitators.[36] They are also to be questioners. The meaning of the Passover (the most important Jewish annual festival) was not to be taught simply by a lecture. It was to be taught *in response to a question* asked by a child who saw the practical effects of the festival in the way his parents were behaving.[37] Training is by example and involves honest answers to questions. It should also be consistent between father and mother. Both father and mother are to be honored, and the "father's instruction" and "law of thy mother" (KJV) are expected to be consistent.[38] If parents give different answers, or one is known to be stricter than the other, then it is confusing and harmful for the child.

Unconditional love, as we have seen, does not imply indulgence, sentimentality, or softness. Sometimes chastisement may be needed. Sometimes also a child has to learn to bear the effects of a misdeed or carelessness. God, too, does not promise to undo all the effects of our sin. Sometimes, indeed, it may be difficult to know when to interfere and when not. This may be especially true in that often difficult phase of adolescence. Problems there encountered may often reflect mistakes made when the child was younger, but can come to any family. The parable of the prodigal son[39] is quite interesting in this respect, for the son was probably about seventeen or eighteen. We note first that the father takes his request seriously, and in fact complies. He has somehow failed to convey to the boy the joys of sharing together, and he does not intend to keep him frustrated and restless at home. He respects his boy's choice. Moreover, he does not try to shield his son from the bad effects of his irresponsibility. Perhaps he failed earlier to train his son to be responsible, but now at least he does not keep on sending extra money to help. It would not really help, but merely prolong the time before the boy "came to himself." The father has every longing for his son to return home, but does not pester him to do so. Yet, when the son does come home, the father does not put his son on trial, or try to rub it in to swell his own ego. His only concern is to reestablish a real relationship, one of sharing which surpasses that which previously existed.

The New Testament reveals to us three distinct phases in a parent-child relationship. The first is when the child is young. At that time he is the heir, and yet in some senses is "no better than a slave."[40] He shares a full relationship with his parents, but is under their discipline without the adult maturity to always understand that discipline or its purposes. He is, of course, a person in every sense of the word, but cannot be treated as a responsible adult. The second phase is entered when a child reaches what the Jews call *"bar mitzvah."* Broadly speaking, this refers to the teen years. In many ways, the son or daughter should now be treated as an adult. They should be able (as with the Jews) to assume more responsible roles in the church. It may become appropriate for other means of discipline to be found than chastisement, such as a loss of privilege. In any case, one suspects that by this time their attitude to authority will already have been formed; and if it is not a healthy one, then beating is unlikely to reform it very easily. The wisdom and benefit of a healthy early training should now be seen.[41] But at this stage, the child is still in his parents' household. Thus, although in some ways an adult, he is still to obey his parents.[42] Thus it was that Jesus at the age of twelve went to his *bar mitzvah* in Jerusalem, and was able at that time to take his place in the adult discussion of the scholars.[43] Yet afterwards he remained obedient to his parents as he remained in their household.[44]

The third stage in parent-child relationships comes in the words, "For this cause shall a man *leave* his father and his mother, and shall cleave to his wife."[45] After this time he should continue to "honor" his father and mother, but is released from the command to "obey" them. Part of that "honor" consists of making provision for any parent in need, especially a widowed mother or grandmother.[46] This is, in a sense, only a return on the parental obligation to provide for children when the dependence was the other way around.[47]

In these days, of course, we are unlike the society in which Jesus lived, in that some people remain always unmarried. To reapply the principles in our context would probably mean, therefore, that someone should obey his or her parents as long as he is under eighteen (our present age of adulthood in law, and a reasonable average age of marriage in ancient Israel), and should obey on questions relating to activity *within* his parents' home for as long as he shares their household. Outside that he is free, and even within those bounds the parents should not "provoke their children to wrath" unnecessarily.

It is interesting to note that the Scriptures never idealize Old Testament characters. We will see in Chapter 11 something of David's less than ideal marital relationships. He was also an ineffectual father. When his eldest son Amnon became depressed, it was not David but his nephew who noticed it. Had David kept a close relationship with his son he might have offered counsel, and if Amnon's feelings proved genuine have arranged a suitable marriage.[48]

Instead Amnon committed rape. David was angry, but did nothing. The Septuagint explains: "But David vexed not the spirit of Amnon his son, because he loved him." David mistook overindulgence for love. He neither punished Amnon, nor comforted Tamar—and Absalom took both upon himself.

David had a doting affection for the good-looking and apparently somewhat vain Absalom,[49] but was apparently not close enough to him to understand the resentment he felt against Amnon.[50] Later David refused to accept the obvious signs in Absalom's behavior that he sought unlawful power.[51] Sadly, after Absalom's rebellion, defeat, and death, his equally good-looking brother Adonijah showed exactly the same signs.[52] In this case, the Scripture actually makes clear the heart of the problem: "His father had never interfered with him by asking, 'Why do you behave as you do?'"[53] David did not discipline his sons, and had not himself shown them a good model of family life.

This should serve us as a warning that even for a "man after God's own heart," family life does not just happen. We need to be conscious of it, to spend time on it, and to make an effort to understand its principles and apply them to our lives.

CHAPTER TEN

Men and Women in the Church Family

Reading: Joel 2:28, 29
1 Timothy 2:11—3:13

It might at first sight seem surprising that a section touching on church order should appear in a book about family relationships. But there is a good reason for this. The word "church" (Greek: *ecclesia*) does not mean an institution, but a group or gathering.[1] The church is the people who make it up. The New Testament, moreover, sees the church as an extension of the family. This is true in two ways. First, fellow-Christians are viewed as brothers and sisters, parents and children, and are to be treated as such.[2] Second, Christian meetings for fellowship and worship tended to be in people's homes, often informally in what was really just an extension of family worship.[3] But if the church is seen in the New Testament as a kind of extension of family, then obviously some of the family relationships will extend into it in some way. In particular, the male/female roles in the family will extend also into the church family. To "preside over" the church family will be a role similar to presiding over one's own family.[4]

Before we look in detail at this, however, it might be useful to think in general about church order. The New Testament contains a fair amount of detail about how the church was governed, and about the format of its gatherings. Not only so, but Paul gives explicit commands as to how these things are to be done, even saying that if anyone is really spiritual he will obey this![5] This means that we should take the New Testament teaching on this very seriously. If we believe in the authority of the Bible, we need to thoroughly understand the principles of church government, order, and gatherings. There may, of course, be *some* aspects which have meaning only in relation to the custom and culture of that day. But they need to be treated as such only after careful examination. Too often major denominations seem to almost totally ignore the New Testament pattern laid down by the apostles and rely instead on tradition or intuition. God will, of course, bless within *any* structure or format whenever he can do so. But he had good reasons for laying down a general pattern in a particular way, and however we may adapt it to circumstances, we should not simply ignore it.

Three words are used for appointed posts in the early church: *episkopos* (bishop); *presbuteros* (elder); and *diakanos* (deacon or minister). The first of these is from a word group meaning to scrutinize or oversee, with overtones in the Septuagint of looking after something.[6] The word *presbuteros* comes from the word for age, but seems to sometimes refer to a recognized group of leaders.[7] The word *diakanos* will be considered later.

The New Testament seems clearly to identify *episkopoi* and *presbuteroi* as the same group of people in the church.[8] Each locality had its one Christian gathering (or "church") in which elders were appointed (or "ordained") under the authority of the apostles.[9] The nature of this recognized appointment may be contrasted with the situation regarding prophets. One became an elder (presumably normally for life) by being appointed to the post. But one became a prophet by receiving and exercising the gift of prophecy from the Holy Spirit, and would be a prophet only as long as one continued to exercise the gift. Paul would not have told Titus to "appoint prophets in every church," for being a prophet was a role rather than an institutional post. A prophet could, of course, exert a great influence, even to the point of having a leadership role, but it would be an inspirational rather than an institutional leadership. It would not be his recognized *responsibility* to lead.

Eldership, then, was a post rather than a function as such. But elders were expected to fulfill three basic leadership roles: to rule or preside, to shepherd, and to teach. It is worth examining these three aspects of their authority.

In chapters 7, 8 we saw that the word *prohistemi* did not mean rule in the sense of a dictatorship, but spoke of a man "presiding over" the creative unit of the family. Elders "preside over" a church in a similar way.[10] Energy, creativity, ideas, ministry, etc. might bubble up from anywhere in the church, as the Holy Spirit inspired it. But the elders, in presiding over the church, had the task of channeling ideas, sifting them, and making any necessary decisions or rulings, which would then be seen as the decision of the church. As the institutionally recognized officers of the church, their decisions were "official policy." But these decisions could well be made with the help of the inspirational influence of nonelders.

Their second function is stated thus: "To the elders among you, I appeal . . . be shepherds of God's flock that is under your care . . . not lording it over those entrusted to you, but being examples to the flock. And when the chief Shepherd appears, you will receive the crown of glory that will never fade away."[11] They are "shepherds" not in any sense of "lordship," but to *lead* the flock by their example. We should remember that Eastern shepherds (then as now) *lead* their sheep; they do not drive them. For this reason, a man appointed to be an elder should be "above reproach.[12] He leads by example. But an Eastern shepherd also carries a "rod,"[13] a symbol of authority. The rod is used to protect the sheep from wolves, and also to redirect any of the flock who are going astray. The authority of the elders may also be a protection by refusing entry to a false prophet (who is like a wolf)[14] and a means to bring back any of the church going astray.

The third eldership function is that they should be "able to teach."[15] This is linked with their rulership: "Let the elders who rule well be considered worthy of double honor, especially those who labour in preaching and teaching."[16] The Greek rendered "doctrine" or "teaching" in the New Testament is the same word. In the New Testament, the title "teacher" implies authority. It was a title often used to address Jesus.[17] And the one under a teacher is a "disciple" rather than merely a "pupil."[18] In the early church, a body of teachings was being laid down by Jesus' chosen apostles; and the church continued steadfastly in "the apostles' teaching."[19] Elders were not originators of doctrine, but an elder should "hold firm to the sound word as taught, so that he may be able to give instruction in sound doctrine and also to confute those who contradict it."[20] Part of the shepherding involved laying down an official line on what should be received as "apostles' doctrine" (KJV). This, clearly, was even more important in the days before the New Testament was compiled. At that time, the elders also had to decide the official line on any new issues. For example, it was a council of leading elders, including the apostles who were also elders,[21] who decided the role of Gentiles in the church.[22] Teaching and authority were very clearly linked.

Yet we must note that the authority of the elders was in no sense a priestly authority. A priest is a human mediator between God and men, and as a special position this ceased with the Old Covenant. The word is never used of a class of people in the church, and its use today is based on misunderstanding. An elder was not a priestly mediator. Neither was he any kind of successor to the twelve apostles and Paul. Their function was one of personal witness to Jesus' resurrection,[23] and their authority was not passed on. (Likewise, the "messengers" sent out by the churches[24] were what we would call "missionaries." They were not successors of the twelve either.) Later church leaders recognized this great distinction between their own authority and that of the twelve apostles and Paul.[25] Elders, then, were neither priests nor successors to the apostles, and there is no biblical evidence that they played any special part in the "breaking of bread" (Communion).

But we need to go further than this. The elders were not even the unique source of spiritual ministry in the church. Spiritual ministry was the function of the Holy Spirit through the whole body of the church. Thus, in a church meeting "each one" present might lead with a psalm, a teaching, a prophecy, etc.[26] In such a gathering, several prophets might speak. Yet what they said must be "weighed" by those present, for though the Spirit might minister through a prophet, the prophet did not have the institutional authority of the elders to lay down church policy.[27] The function of elders was not to monopolize spiritual ministry, but to make sure that the church in general stayed along the right lines, and to decide church policy and doctrine. But the modern system in many denominations, where spiritual ministry is virtually concentrated in one full-time minister, is quite foreign to the New Testament.

In most denominations, this lack of New Testament pattern complicates the discussion of the place of women in the ministry. Those of us who wish the debate to be based on the revelation of God, rather than on, say, the value of tradition or the supposed psychological fitness or unfitness of women, have special problems in this respect. It is, of course, meaningless in biblical terms to ask if a woman can be ordained a priest, when there is no human class of priests in the church as God sees it. But even in many nonconformist groups, the pattern of ministry differs from that laid down as binding under apostolic authority.[28] Since no counterpart existed in the New Testament church to the minister as conceived by many modern groups, it again becomes impossible to say whether (according to God's revelation in Scripture) a woman can be a "minister." If we really want to take the Bible as our authority, we need to strive (whatever our particular denomination or tradition) to get closer to the divinely revealed pattern for church order and ministry, in which the relative roles of men and women is just one aspect.

We may bear this background in mind as we consider the words of the Apostle Paul: "Let a woman learn in silence with all submissiveness. I permit no woman to teach or to have authority over men; she is to keep silent."²⁹ What does this mean? Let us note carefully Paul's words. Women are to learn (literally) "in subjection." As we have seen, God's family pattern of wives "in subjection" to their husbands extends also to the family of the church. So what should it imply? It would mean that just as the woman cannot be the institutionally recognized presider over the marriage unit, so she cannot be the institutionally recognized presider over the church unit. She cannot hold eldership. For her to do so would mean she was in subjection to her husband in family matters, while he was in subjection to her in church matters. The apostles knew no such division between church and family life.

Paul confirms that this is his meaning by using the phrase, "teach and have authority." This is, as we have seen, a job description of an elder. Not, of course, that *all* teaching is forbidden to women, for Paul speaks of some teaching roles for women.³⁰ It is specifically the eldership role of laying down authoritative doctrines of the church that is forbidden to women. Paul gives this as his own ruling for the churches, and this leaves it open as to whether there might be exceptional or different circumstances in which some other course could be the best. But the reasons for it are fundamental ones, based on God's normal revealed design for family life.

To expand on this, Paul goes back to the beginnings of family and community life in Eden: "For Adam was formed first, then Eve; and Adam was not deceived, but the woman was deceived and became a transgressor. Yet woman will be saved through bearing children...."³¹ Eve was a "helper" for Adam, meaning an ally and an equal. But Paul notes how Adam is portrayed as being formed first, and Eve as formed out of and through Adam.³² In fact, in the

Genesis account God is shown giving the moral command to Adam before Eve was created, and first requiring Adam to answer for it.[33] Paul sees this as illustrating the institutional leadership of man in marriage. Yet, as we know, both Adam and Eve ignored it. Eve chose to follow the serpent's advice rather than follow what Adam had told her was God's instruction, and she evidently did it without even discussing it with him. Then Adam chose to follow his wife's lead in eating the fruit, and tried to escape his own God-given responsibility by blaming her afterwards.[34] However much of the account we take to be allegorical, it is clear that something is involved of both man and woman trying to reject the pattern of institutional responsibility implicitly laid down by God. In the church order, Paul wants no such thing. The male elders must face up to their own institutional responsibility (whoever's lead they may choose to follow) for laying down doctrine. The women know clearly that God has chosen to let authoritative teaching be established in *this* way, and are neither to listen to other voices nor seek to usurp authority for themselves.

We should note several things here. First, Paul nowhere says that women are unfit to be elders. He does not say that women are more likely to be deceived than men. His reference to Genesis is a purely historical one, showing that attempts to reject a God-given pattern led to disaster. This does not depend on any supposed universal characteristics of men and women.

Second, Paul himself was evidently concerned that no one should misunderstand him to be saying that women are inferior. In one passage, he goes on to emphasize that the human race is a unity, for though Eve was formed out of and through Adam, men come out of and through their mothers.[35] In the Timothy

MEN AND WOMEN IN THE CHURCH FAMILY

passage he is more explicit: "But she shall be saved through the childbearing, if they continue in faith, love and sanctification with sobriety."[36] This again refers to the unity of the human race, but seems to refer back to the next part of the Genesis story. The serpent (which Paul takes as an allegorical reference to Satan)[37] will be crushed by the seed of the woman. God in Genesis chose to emphasize the special part that woman (through Mary) would play in bringing Christ into the world. Paul's reference to "*the* childbearing" must surely refer to this, for to take it literally would imply that a childless woman could not be saved, which would be an absurd doctrine to ascribe to Paul.

Third, we should note what Paul immediately passes on to say. He lists the characteristics (married men of long Christian experience and high moral standing) necessary for those ruling and teaching as elders.[38] This reaffirms the point that in forbidding women to "teach ... to usurp authority" (KJV), he has in mind the institutional authority of eldership. The passage also implies the reason for restricting eldership to men: "If anyone does not know how to manage his own family, how can he take care of God's church?"[39] As we have said, early Christians met in people's homes, and the church was an extension of family. Thus, the man's role in the church was an extension of that in his family.

None of this, of course, is based on any supposed inadequacy of women to act as elders. It is simply based on the churchly implications of God's divinely revealed order for families. We can see good reasons why God might establish such a clear unambiguous order for families, but they are reasons of unambiguity rather than any supposed inadequacy of women.

We should also note exactly what is forbidden to

women. It is the institutional authority of eldership. But women, both in church and in family, may exercise inspirational leadership. In other words, her husband (or a church) may recognize that she possesses particular wisdom on some matter and may follow her advice. This does not cancel the male responsibility for the decision, but it is a valid function of being a "helper" or a fellow-worker.[40] We find that the Bible often alludes to such inspirational leadership. Perhaps the function of the savior-judge Deborah could be seen in this light.[41] Such women judges were not recognized in an institutional way as kings, but held power in the manner of a prophet,[42] by their inspirational leadership. Likewise, the wise woman who saved her city Abel by her influence with Joab and her people had no institutional authority, but was listened to because of her inspirational leadership.

Paul, who based his views of women consciously on the Old Testament,[43] would not have wished to overthrow this kind of role for women. He appreciated the work of Priscilla in sharing with her husband equally in the exposition of Christian truth to the church leader Apollos early in his work.[44] He also refers to a woman, Phoebe, as a minister or deacon *(diakonon)* of the Cenchrean church. He tells the Roman church to assist her, and says that she had been a "helper" *(prostatis)* of many, including himself."[45] The word *prostatis* is not used anywhere else in the New Testament, but is used five times in the Greek Old Testament to mean "ruler" or "officer."[46] In general Greek literature, it meant "leader," "patron," "protector" (the defender of an inferior!).[47] This is the word Paul, an *apostle,* uses to describe Phoebe's relationship with himself! Certainly this was a position of importance and influence, though again, of course, it was not one of institutional ruling authority.

We might pause to note at this point that there was another institutional post in the New Testament church which did not carry the ruling authority of eldership. Just as the word "messenger" *(apostolos)* assumed a technical sense in some contexts, so the word "minister" *(diakonos)* seems in places to refer to a specific post.[48] The kind of people required were broadly the same, but the phrase "an apt teacher"[49] is omitted, for teaching carries overtones of eldership authority. The exact functions of deacons are uncertain, but many people associate them with those appointed in Acts 6, where the verbal form of *diakoneo* is used.[50] If so, it would imply that the social work and famine relief undertaken by the seven later became the work of recognized deacons. Phoebe may have been one of these, and the context of 1 Timothy 3:11 seems to make best sense if we take Paul to be referring there to lady deacons. Unlike elders who were chosen for spiritual authority by those with spiritual insight,[51] the seven deacons were elected by the people.[52] Probably this was for the practical purpose that to counter complaints about unfairness,[53] they themselves should choose the men.

On the practical level, one should also point out the apparent importance of the houses owned by women for early church meetings. After Pentecost, Peter evidently knew that the most important prayer meeting would be taking place at a woman's house.[54] Paul used Lydia's house as a base for mission.[55] Nymphas evidently had a church meeting in her house.[56] The reference to "Chloe's people" as a trusted source of information may indicate a sound group in Chloe's house.[57] Considering the few references to such things, the predominance of women is noticeable.

As far as women's participation in the life of the

church was concerned, Paul forbade them to teach authoritatively, but allowed them to give exegesis[58] and to prophesy.[59] The word "prophesy" is an often misunderstood Greek word, really meaning not just predicting the future, but "forthtelling" God's message.[60] Unlike authoritative teaching, not all prophecy must be accepted; but it must be weighed spiritually against known truth.[61] The Jews expected both men and women to prophesy,[62] and God's promise of the New Covenant made it clear that the increase in prophecy due to the Spirit was to be shared equally between men and women.[63] It was part of God's foretold New Covenant design. So, for example, the four unmarried daughters of one of the seven respected and Spirit-filled deacons were recognized as prophetesses in the early church.[64]

Thus, it was quite normal for Paul to refer in 1 Corinthians 11 to women leading public worship in prayer or prophecy. Paul makes it clear that this is the context he has in mind by his words, "if anyone ... we recognize no other practice, nor do the *churches* of God." Paul does not say, "*church* of God," but "*churches* of God." The word *churches* really means gatherings; so Paul is saying that it is normal custom in church gatherings for women to pray and prophesy with covered heads.

Now this must form the background as we try to understand the admittedly difficult comment on women which appears later in Paul's letter.[65] Many take it to mean that women cannot pray or prophesy in church gatherings, nor lead public worship. We find this interpretation impossible for several reasons. First, it would be very odd for Paul to refer in Chapter 11 to a normal church practice of women praying and prophesying with covered heads, but then forbid them to pray or prophesy at all in Chap-

MEN AND WOMEN IN THE CHURCH FAMILY 117

ter 14. It has been argued that Paul wanted to deal with one topic at a time. But then, surely, in Chapter 11 he would simply have said, "It is a shame for a woman to appear in church with unveiled head," whereas he deliberately says that the practice in churches is for them to lead worship.

Second, Paul seems to connect his forbidding them to speak with their being "in submission." A woman who is leading public worship can remain subject; ministry and authority are two entirely different things. Old Testament prophetesses who made public prophecy were not thereby refusing to be subject to their husbands.

Third, some people have connected Paul's words, "as the Law says," with women literally being in silence. But neither biblical law, nor even rabbinical oral law forbade the woman to speak in a synagogue. According to rabbinical law women were forbidden to *teach*,[66] but could be called to the readiing of the Torah in the synagogue (though in practice they were not).[67]

Fourth, Paul's illustration of what he means—"If there is anything they desire to know, let them ask their husbands at home"[68]—simply does not relate to a woman leading worship in prayer and prophecy.

Last, it is hard to imagine Paul giving an instruction which he insists is a commandment of Jesus rooted in the essential origins of the gospel,[69] but which would fundamentally contradict the New Covenant prophecy that both the sons and daughters of Israel would prophesy.

Now this means that, however we look at the verses, we surely cannot interpret them to be a literal ban on all speaking. In actual fact, practically no one today would take literally Paul's words, "they are not permitted to speak." The word "speak" is *laleō*, and in another passage describing a church gathering, this is shown to include "psalms and hymns and spiritual songs."[70] In other words, if we took all this literally, the women would not be allowed to sing either. But in this connection, nearly everyone agrees that the *context* of the word "speak" must explain its meaning, restricting its areas of application. All that we are saying is that a more detailed look at the context (particularly bearing in mind also what has gone before) indicates a greater restriction in the area of application than some others would believe.

The context of the passage is a general rebuke to the Corinthians for the disorderliness of their meetings. Their basic trouble was a "do your own thing" mentality. Their Communion service was evidently a shambles, with people eating at different times, overeating, and even getting drunk.[71] In their worship meetings, there was a hubbub of confused noises as people all spoke in tongues and prophesied at the same time, as they felt inclined.[72] Evidently some people felt that the "spiritual man" (verse 37) should not curtail any form of free expression or individual action. Paul opposed this, because God is a God of order, not of tumult.[73] There is also a God-given order of things represented in the word *hupotasso* (subjection), which really means "to set in order under." The spirits of the prophets are "set in order under" the prophets; thus, it is wrong for a man (claiming to be spiritual) to say, "If the spirit moves me, I *must* speak immediately." The women are "set in order under" the elders and, again, should only speak in a proper context. This emphasis on proper order implies that in certain contexts, people should hold their peace. This is the meaning of the word *sigao*,[74] which is a different word from that Paul used in 1 Timothy 2. It means to keep something to oneself. Someone with a "tongue" should keep it to himself unless there is an interpreter (verse 28). Someone prophesying should keep it to himself if another has a more urgent desire to speak (verse 30). And the women, if they have questions, should keep them to themselves until a more suitable time (verse 34).

Unfortunately we have to remind ourselves that we are looking here at only half of a correspondence. The Corinthians had written to ask Paul a number of specific questions,[75] to which he replied in this letter. They had evidently asked him about spiritual gifts and worship meetings.[76] What exactly had been raised with respect to women in meetings, we simply do not know. It is possible that in Corinth they sat segregated from the men at this time, for some early churches may have followed the synagogue pattern in this. But what kind of talking had been reported to Paul, we can never be sure. Paul's words cannot be taken at literal face value for three reasons.

First, as we have seen, the word "speak" (14:34) would then include singing as well, which no one believes. Second, in verse 31 Paul had said that *all* should *learn* from the prophecy in meetings. Thus, his words, "If there is *anything* they desire to *know*, let them ask their husbands at home" (verse 35), would contradict this if taken literally. Third, this would not legislate for widows in the church. Widows made their own decisions, without being subject to anyone in the family,[77] and had no husband "at home" to ask. So Paul must have intended the Corinthians to intelligently interpret his words in the light of their practices, which unfortunately we cannot now know.

But none of it seems to concern leading worship in prayer or prophecy. A woman who did this recognized her position as a married woman (in that society) by covering her hair, and this sign itself became her "authority" to lead public worship.[78] She did not wish to "learn" anything; she was not asking questions, but letting the Spirit minister through her. Paul's comment seems to concern questions, but we cannot now be sure what exactly these were. It is possible that Paul's teaching to "let the others weigh what is said" by the prophets[79] implied a verbal discussion. This might have led to the women reaching their own consensus, rather than relying on the elders for doctrinal direction. Again, it may be that the women of Corinth were discussing and questioning the decisions of the elders. Women today sometimes discuss church affairs and discipline after meetings (often more so in groups who bar women from useful work of ministry). In Corinth, the meetings were evidently so chaotic that this could have happened during the meetings themselves. This would make sense of Paul's words: be subject; hold your peace; discuss church decisions with your husbands (or at least with those more familiar with the considerations), not with other ladies in a group.

However these two controversial verses are taken, there are difficulties of interpretation. No one can really take them literally, and their meanings must relate to the (to us) unknown context. There is all the more audacity, then, in those who try to use these two verses to effectively bar half the church of Christ from any active ministry of the Spirit. From our own view, we believe that this is sadly mistaken and that the interpretation is along something like the lines which we have suggested. The essential message is that church decisions should be discussed quietly between husband and wife, not subject to criticism and questioning in a context where the more influential women meet together. Ironically, those churches who do bar women from spiritual ministry do not seem to lessen this latter problem. The elders' wives quite often (in such groups) exercise offstage iron control, preventing any movement under the Spirit's direction to new blessings.

How can we apply these various principles and ideas in the churches today? We have already noted that the function of Christ's apostles was to witness to his life and resurrection from firsthand experience, and this could not be passed on.[80] The supreme authority of the apostles, therefore, as distinct from the authority of ordinary "apostles of the churches" or "missionaries," died with them. Thus, the "apostles' doctrine,"[81] which the early church had firsthand, is available to us only through the New Testament Scriptures written under the apostles' authority. But this obviously means that unlike the early church, we cannot settle any disputes by direct appeal to the apostles for judgment. In this respect, our church structure can never follow completely the New Testament practice. If we regard as mistaken the attempts of various rival groups to set up their leaders as successors to Christ's apostles, we must simply accept this fact.

At a local level, however, we may follow the New Testament pattern fairly closely. The structures set up at that time related to the nature of the New Covenant, not to any cultural factors peculiar to that day. As a matter of fact, the cultures of areas into which the gospel first came were at least as varied as ours today. Let us, therefore, look at the organization of the local church. Remember that elders were neither priests, nor those who necessarily led the worship. Their role was to "rule." They were institutionally recognized leaders, making day to day decisions on policy and church discipline as well as laying down a teaching program. In many modern denominations, it is difficult to see who exactly is fulfilling the eldership role. In some, ironically, women do sit on the ruling bodies, but may not be "ordained." But it would seem that (following a New Testament pattern) a woman should not occupy an institutional position of ruling authority in a church. This conclusion cannot simply be written off as cultural prejudice of the first century. As we have seen, for a woman to hold institutional authority in the church would conflict with being subject to her husband within the family. Once we see both the logic and authority of God's order for the family, the church order follows.

One might argue that a widow or spinster might hold such authority. Adult spinsters were, of course, virtually unknown in Paul's day, but there does seem to be evidence that there was some kind of appointed position of "widow."[82] What it was, we do not know. But the problem with conferring eldership authority on a spinster or widow is that they could later marry. There may, of course, be special circumstances where the rules, so to speak, are best broken. Paul gives the ruling as for his churches,[83] and it is possible that a situation could be so demonstrably different that for a woman to rule would be the best thing in spite of any possible family life problems.

This leaves many functions open to both men and women. A woman can still be a minister in a full-time capacity. Properly speaking, the ministry is the work of the Holy Spirit through the whole body of the church. But it is not wrong to speak of male and female ministers (like Phoebe). This is true whether they are full-time or (like Paul) have a secular occupation as well. Spiritual ministry does not imply authority or government.

If we follow New Testament practice, we should

allow such ministry to include prophecy (which may include much of which we would now call preaching). Women could expound Scripture (as did Priscilla). Women could lead public worship in prayer. Women could also teach in various situations,[84] as directed under the elders' authority. This would not be to "usurp authority,"[85] but to recognize it.

Let us hope that our churches of all traditions come to recognize again the great potential for spiritual ministry in "ordinary" members. Men and women, without holding institutional posts of authority, may be used by the Spirit to minister. We might look more for the kind of husband-wife teamwork of Aquila and Priscilla which evidently impressed Paul. We should look more for women like Lydia, like Phoebe, who worked as Paul's honored fellow-laborers. Then, perhaps, the prophecy will be realized: *"The Lord gives the word. The women that publish the tidings are a great host."*[86]

CHAPTER ELEVEN

Marriage Problems and Divorce

Readings: Matthew 19:3-12; Mark 10:2-12
Ephesians 5:21-33

Our starting point here will be to look at the biblical approach to divorce. We need to distinguish between God's ideal at which we should aim, and God's realism in situations which are less than ideal.

God stated clearly his plans in Genesis 2. A man and a woman who have become "one flesh" through marriage would surely need a drastic "surgical" operation to separate them. This is how we should see divorce. Yet the first recorded divorce in the Bible was under God's direct guidance! Why? God had promised Abraham many descendants, but by the time he was eighty-five he was still childless. His wife Sarah therefore gave her maid Hagar "to Abram her husband as a wife."[1] Later, after first Hagar and then Sarah herself had borne Abraham sons, there was much bitterness and rivalry between the two women and their offspring.[2] So Sarah said to Abraham, "*Cast out* this slave woman with her son; for the son of this slave woman shall not be heir with my son Isaac."[3]

MARRIAGE PROBLEMS AND DIVORCE

The word rendered "cast out" is the imperative form of a Hebrew word *(garash)*, elsewhere used for divorce. Abraham was unwilling to divorce Hagar, but God said, "Do as she tells you, for through Isaac shall your descendants be named."[4] Abraham divorced Hagar on God's guidance.

Does God, then, approve divorce? No. But we must recognize that this was *already* a less than ideal situation. Abraham had become a polygamist without God's approval. His wife nagged him into it, and then blamed him afterwards when things began to go wrong![5] Hagar despised Sarah, who beat her.[6] Sarah may have been obedient,[7] but was hardly the perfect wife. Then Ishmael mocked Isaac.[8] Moreover, Ishmael was the eldest and so should have been chief heir, which had not been God's intention. In short, Abraham's family affairs were in a total mess. It was in this situation that God saw divorce as the *least of the evils*. We note that Abraham never *disobeyed* God's direct commands, and never ceased to be in a relationship with God. Abraham was not written off as a wicked sinner beyond reprieve. He was a giant of faith in some senses.[9] Yet, God told him to get divorced. This too should guide our attitudes. God is a realist.

The Mosaic Law introduces the subject thus: "When a man takes a wife and marries her, if then she finds no favor in his eyes because he has found some indecency in her, and he writes her a bill of divorce...."[10] This rendering is the most generally accepted, and it implies that it is not a law introducing divorce, nor even suggesting it. It is a law to restrict certain practices surrounding an already existing custom. It is presumed that, on the man's action, if not initiative, the woman can be divorced. It also presumes that she can and may remarry; there is no concept of divorce in order to stay unmarried. In fact, it presumes that the man will have to give her a "bill of divorce," the purpose of which seems simply to *enable* her to remarry. A woman cast out (like Hagar) without any proof that she had been legally divorced would be unable to remarry. So the bill was for her benefit and protection, providing for possible remarriage. But all this is incidental to the passage. Its actual point is to forbid her original husband to take her back again if she has been married to another man in the meantime.

Other laws similarly regulate the practice. One law says that a man (like Abraham) divorcing an ex-slave could not resell her, but must let her go free.[11] Another law says that a man with two wives must (unlike Abraham) give the double portion of inheritance to the firstborn son, irrespective of which wife bore him.[12] There were laws forbidding a man to divorce if he had been made to marry after seducing the woman, or if he had wrongly accused her of not being a virgin on their wedding night.[13] This, perhaps, was because these might indicate that he was an unwilling spouse!

We have considered one divorcé—Abraham. We might now look at an adulterer, polygamist, murderer, and divorcé—David. His first wife was Princess Michal, who fell madly in love with him.[14] When times became difficult for David, he deserted her[15] and took other wives.[16] Michal, evidently considered divorced from David, became the wife of a man called Palti.[17] The Scripture itself calls Palti her "husband," and so the new marriage was presumably legally valid.[18] Under the Mosaic Law, therefore, Michal was divorced from David and remarried, and David was strictly forbidden to take her back as his wife again.[19] This, as we know, is precisely what

David *did* do when he came to power, to her legal husband's evident distress. David reclaimed her as his "wife,"[20] but Scripture itself refers to her thereafter not as the "wife of David,"[21] but as the "daughter of Saul."[22] David had perhaps committed the "abomination unto the Lord" of divorce and remarriage to the same woman, forbidden in Deuteronomy.

Later, David committed adultery with the wife of a man away fighting for him, and in fear of discovery had the man murdered.[23] The punishment for this, of course, should have been death. But no one, not even God, suggested it. God instead sent Nathan to touch David's shepherd-heart and conscience at its most tender point, and David repented of this at least.[24] Yet, even after this David decided to continue his liaison with the woman. He made her his queen, although he was already married. He gave her son Solomon the inheritance rights of the firstborn, although forbidden in the Mosaic Law to do so.[25] Yet God (after punishing David) accepted this arrangement and Solomon as king.

We see, of course, that not all the effects of David's sins could be removed. In this area especially the "sins of the fathers are visited on the children," for they learn wrong approaches to relationships from their parents. Thus, David's son Amnon raped his half-sister and then spurned her; David could say nothing after his own scandalous conduct. And another son, Absalom, later took the law into his own hands.[26] Absalom also broke the law by taking his father's wives.[27] Much later, the downfall of Solomon himself was through matrimonial problems.[28] God does not stop all the effects of our sins. But he does accept practicalities. In some circumstances he may accept divorce as the best alternative; and on the other hand, he may accept and bless a real *de facto* present marriage in spite of a very shady origin of the liaison. There is, moreover, no indication that a couple with a less than ideal past are therefore barred from any future work for God. Neither Abraham after his divorce, nor David after retaking his ex-wife Michal were barred from service to God. God is more merciful and less doctrinaire than some of his followers seem to be.

There is little else about divorce in the Old Testament. In one context, all the people are encouraged by Ezra to divorce their pagan wives.[29] In another context, God says that he hates divorce.[30] Divorce is never ideal, but in some situations it may be the least of the evils.

The grounds for divorce were never laid down in the Old Testament. The phrase used incidentally in Deuteronomy 24:1 ("indecent") is literally "nakedness of a thing." This occurs only twice in Scripture and is obscure in meaning. By Jesus' time, there were two schools of thought on its meaning. That of Hillel took it to mean anything which brought shame, including quarreling or burning the lunch! The school of Shammai restricted it to adultery as the sole grounds. This is the background of the question to Jesus: "Is it lawful to divorce one's wife for *any* cause?"[31] The accounts in the Gospels are not identical, and it seems clear that we do not have a verbatim report of the incident. But the teaching of Jesus which emerges is this. First, Genesis says that husband and wife become one flesh; Jesus took this to mean that they are no longer two but one. The termination of a marriage, therefore, does not merely imply a legal enactment of divorce. It involves a splitting of a *real* as well as a legal union. Man should not *separate* what God intended to remain as one unit.[32]

The Pharisees asked him why, therefore, Moses had *commanded* them to divorce. Jesus replied that Moses had *allowed* divorce because of their hardness of heart.[33]

In other words, there was divine recognition (as we have already seen) that in some circumstances, in a less than ideal world, divorce was the least of the evils. But it had always been God's intention for marriage to be a permanent commitment. It was this kind of thinking, more basic perhaps than the legalistic arguments of the school of Shammai, which led Jesus to a serious view of divorce. It was not something to be considered lightly—and certainly not for trivialities like burnt lunch. It was to be considered only for serious "immorality."[34] The word Jesus actually used is *not* the word for adultery *(moicheia)*, but a more general word *(porneia)*.[35] It seems unlikely, therefore, that he intended a strictly legalistic restriction to only one ground of divorce (namely, adultery). The word *porneia* is often used in a figurative sense, but it certainly does mean some serious fault.

First, however, note how Jesus drew out a further implication of the Genesis teaching that marriage involved a one-flesh unity. There could be no vestige of a double standard. A husband divorcing his wife is to be seen in the same light as a wife divorcing her husband.[36] Jewish practice had never permitted women to initiate divorce, and neither did the Greeks. Under Roman law, however, the form of marriage—normal for over a century before Jesus' ministry—could be dissolved by either partner. No grounds were needed, and divorce and remarriage of Romans was very common indeed.[37] It is certain, therefore, that the idea of woman divorcing man would be familiar at that time, and Jesus deliberately states the issue generally. Jesus also implied that the remarriage of either man or woman after an unjustifiable divorce was on a level with adultery.[38] This went far beyond the Mosaic legal code, which regulated but did not forbid either polygamy or free remarriage of divorcées of either sex. This astonished Jesus' disciples. In fact, it had on them the effect Jesus evidently intended; it made them realize how seriously the marriage commitment should be taken. So stunned were they that they wondered if it was therefore too much of a risk getting married at all![39]

We should note, incidentally, that this was no armchair philosophy. Herodias and Herod Antipas had both divorced to marry each other, and John the Baptist had been murdered for his criticism of this.[40] Jesus' words about women divorcing could (in a society where this was rare) have been taken as an allusion to Herodias; so Jesus risked a death like John the Baptist's.

How should Jesus' words be interpreted practically? Should the church regard all remarried divorcées as living in sin? Should a divorcée be discouraged from remarriage? Are there "justifiable grounds" for divorce? What many people seem to seek is a kind of rule book to meet all circumstances. But this is utterly mistaken. God did not operate divorce in such a way even in the Old Covenant, which had the Law; so why should he do so for those who are not under the Law, but under grace?

Let us, however, try to see where a rule book approach to Jesus' words would lead us. A strictly legalistic approach would presumably imply that anyone who divorces (except perhaps for adultery) is living in an adulterous union if he or she later remarries. Let us see the implications of this.

First, note that the word "adultery" means unfaithfulness of a *married* person. If a divorcée's new marriage union is adulterous, then it must presumably be because (in the eyes of God) he or she is still married to the original partner. If so, then it must surely be right for him (or her) to return to that original partner and live as married. This makes a nice tidy sense of Jesus' words, seen as a set of rules. Unfortunately, it directly contradicts God's words in Deuteronomy (24:1-4). He says that for a remarried divorcée to return to the original partner is an abomination. In fact, it is one of the few points God makes about divorce in the Old Testament, so he must have felt strongly about it. But Jesus was surely interpreting Deuteronomy, not contradicting it.

A second absurdity with the rule-book approach is this. Suppose that a couple divorce (not for *porneia*), and both remarry other partners. Under a rule book, when they both form their new liaisons, both are adulterous. But (according to a rule book) adultery is a valid grounds for divorce. Therefore, their divorce becomes valid, and so their new unions are no longer adulterous. But this kind of pettifogging is more like the worst aspects of the Rabbis than the living and pragmatic approach of God in the Old Testament.

There is a third absurdity. If we take Jesus' words to be establishing a new rule book, then we must look carefully at the whole sermon where he first introduces this new ruling on divorce.[41] In another part of it he says, "Every one who looks at a woman lustfully *has* already *committed adultery* with her in his heart."[42] If this is also part of our new rule book, then presumably lust counts the same as adultery under the rules, and a single incidence of such lust is an adequate grounds for divorce. In this case, one suspects that many Christian wives would have grounds to divorce their husbands.

There is a fourth sense in which the legalistic approach is absurd. Let us consider the reaction of a legalistic church to two applications for membership. Miss Take married a man who was unkind to her. She divorced, remarried, and had two children by the second husband. She and her second husband then became Christians and now seek church membership. The legalistic church must refuse, for her divorce was not strictly for adultery; so they see her present union as adulterous. In order to become a church member, she would have to split her present family and leave her two children without one parent and with a broken home. Alternatively, she and her husband might be admitted as some species of spiritual leper—on a level of those living in sin, and so to be given no spiritual work.

On the other hand, Miss Use lived in sin with two men for ten years without getting married. She then left both to marry a third. Afterwards the couple became Christians and now seek church membership. The legalistic church will receive them (provided that they repent of former sins) as full and honored members of the church. Whatever her past conduct, her present marriage is valid as she is not divorced. Amazingly, this kind of legalism would often be applied by Christians to keep a consistent witness, but in our view it is the kind of consistency God would prefer not to have.

In our view, therefore, the rule-book approach is misguided. We should rather begin from a distinction between the pre- and post- situations. If Abraham had asked God whether to marry Hagar, God would surely have said no, for Hagar (as Paul tells us[43]) was a fleshly idea to try to fulfill God's promises. Abraham should and could have avoided his marital mess; but *after* it had arisen, God saw divorce as the least of the evils. When we are *contemplating* a course of action, God will set before us his ideal. *After* we have taken a wrong course of action, God is more concerned about picking up the pieces in the best way possible.

Likewise with David. As David contemplated adultery, then murder, then marriage to the widow, God would have held up before David his ideal. But *after* David had committed all these things, God accepted the marriage as an active ongoing union and made the best of the situation. Neither Abraham nor David were thereafter regarded as spiritual lepers.

Jesus, in our view, holds up God's ideal to men tempted to seek divorce lightly and for selfish reasons. Marriage is a one-flesh unit, meant to last until dissolved by one partner's death. The breakup of the marriage unit is, as we saw in Chapter 2, blasphemous because it breaks a unit reflecting the unity of the Godhead; it is antisocial because it breaks a social unit; it is antifamily because it leaves a conflict of loyalties in the children. So God hates divorce. To split a one-flesh unit is, like any surgery, a drastic measure. If a couple have marital problems, then they should be encouraged to try to solve them with God's help. Divorce is not a thing to be lightly approached or considered. But, nevertheless, God recognizes the realities of situations. In some circumstances, the reality of marriage as God intended it has already gone. This is not a question of vague feelings, like the old cry, "I just don't love her/him any more." Marriage is not based on feelings, but on settled attitudes. Neither is it a question of trivial irritations like burnt lunch. The marriage dies when the relationship is fundamentally broken down. In such circumstances, a divorce may be little more than a legal enactment of what is already a reality. It comes at a point where it is obvious that the marriage is not going to be reestablished. No one can provide a rule book to say exactly when that point is reached. Jesus' word *porneia* is a vague but serious word. It is a matter for spiritual discernment, pastoral counseling, and personal decision. God gave Abraham the pastoral counseling he wanted—without hiding behind a rule book of generalities. God's pastoral assistants now are the church leaders or elders.[44] They should not duck their responsibilities.

What about our attitudes to those in a post-situation? How should we treat divorcés like Abraham or David, whether remarried or not? First, we should make sure that our attitude is one of love and concern. It is all too easy to cast the first stone at adulterers. Yet, by Jesus' definition, one suspects that most of the men in our churches are adulterous at one time or another[45] and deserve death under the Law. This is not, of course, to excuse sin. But we should recognize that the fundamental sin is in the breakup of the first marriage relationship. We do not mean by this the legal divorce, but the breakup of the *relationship*. It is here that there may be some need for repentance, especially if the breakup was largely due to the divorcé now seeking acceptance into a church fellowship. This is something which would have to be discussed seriously with the elders in that church. But it is here that the question lies. We cannot believe that the God of Abraham and Isaac would want the church to try to break up a committed marriage relationship in the present because of what happened in the past. Neither can we believe that a person who has had a marriage break up in the past is automatically barred from seeking a life partner in the present. This is simply not how God operates.

Now some may say that this approach opens the door to license. This does not alarm us, for the same kind of thing was said of Paul. Legalists misunderstood Paul to be saying that it was all right to sin because God would forgive.[46] Perhaps they may misunderstand us to be saying that marriage breakup is all right, because God will favor the best practical solution to heal the broken pieces afterwards. But the difference between liberty and license is this: Liberty is when our freedom from the letter of the Law is used to seek God's best solution in a situation; license is when our freedom from regulations is used to indulge selfish desires with no thought of seeking God's will. It is a question of heart and motive which distinguishes the gospel of grace and love from a false gospel of abuse and lust. There are certainly cases today where church discipline should be applied. But God's chosen authority in pastoral care (the elders) cannot avoid their responsibility. They must seek God's guidance through the Spirit in dealing with any difficult cases of marital confusion or divorce. They cannot hide behind a rule book.

We have been thinking about Jesus' teaching on marriage and divorce. What of Paul? Various attempts to view Paul's words on the subject as a new legal code are doomed to failure. Paul was simply not thinking legalistically. Thus, for example, he says that a woman is "bound by *law*" to her husband until death.[47] What law? Both the Mosaic and the Jewish oral law (not to mention Greek, Roman, etc.) allowed divorce in some circumstances—which made the woman "freed from the law of her husband."[48] As a strict legal pronouncement on existing law, Paul's statement would be wrong. If, on the other hand, he were making *new* legislation he would surely not ascribe it to "law." Rather, we must take him to be speaking generally and ideally, not strictly legalistically.

The same is true of the well-known 1 Corinthians 7 passage. This seems based on Jesus' words, "What God has joined together, let man not *separate*."[49] By "separate" Jesus meant the dissolution of marriage, emphasizing the surgical splitting of the marriage union rather than the purely legal aspect of divorce. Unlike some theologians, he did not, of course, say that man *cannot* separate such a union. Nor is it stated as an inflexible rule, for he has already given the exception for *porneia*.

Paul paraphrases Jesus: "I enjoin, not I but the Lord, let not a wife be *separated* from her husband."[50] Paul intends this (as did Jesus) as an ideal rather than an inflexible rule, for his second instruction which follows is: "But if indeed she separates, let her remain unmarried or to her husband be reconciled."[51] If they were absolutely never to separate, then why would Paul go on to give instructions on how to do it? Taken strictly legalistically, this second instruction contradicts both Jesus' words and Paul's own first instruction. Ironically, some have not only failed to note this, but have gone on to elevate the *second* instruction into an inflexible legal code. Paul's concern here, however, is not legal enactment, but with aiming at the best in less than ideal situations.

We need also remember that Paul is here answering specific questions they had asked.[52] It is easy to guess some of these. Corinth was a society rife with immorality, prostitution, and idolatry. How could a newly-converted woman live a pure life while living with a husband who regularly got drunk, visited brothels, and worshiped idols? Surely she should leave him? After all, God encouraged Old Testament

MARRIAGE PROBLEMS AND DIVORCE

believers to *divorce* their pagan spouses[53] and the Jewish oral law enjoined *divorce* if a spouse left Judaism.[54] What did Paul think? Surely they should at least set up a separate household, even if not actually divorced?

Paul begins by setting up the ideal of Jesus: "let man not separate." This makes it clear that he regards the marriage as no less valid because the wedding was a pagan one. But the comment Paul adds about *how* to separate indicates that he does not take this legalistically. He then goes on to give his own advice on how to act in their particular circumstances. Christian renouncement of the "world" is inner and spiritual—not a physical separation as with Israel. Thus, the Christian is *not* defiled in "dwelling with" a pagan spouse (verses 12, 13, KJV). Paul says that they should not "leave" their partner—the word used meaning to "abandon" rather than "separate" the marriage union.[55]

Paul then continues, "But if the unbelieving partner desires to *separate,* let it be so; in such a case the brother or sister is not bound."[56] This refers not merely to abandoning, but to "separation" of the marriage union. What does "separation" mean here? It certainly did not mean a kind of legal category such as we know today. Paul cannot be inventing a new kind of legal category, for the context is one of what the *pagan* partner sought. No legal category of separation different from divorce existed in Jewish, Greek, or Roman law; and no pagan partner would or could seek such a state. Paul uses the word "separation" (as had Jesus) to emphasize the ending of the union, rather than the legal aspect of divorce. The particular legal code under which they were married (and so the legal aspects of divorce) do not concern him. He focuses on the reality, not the law.

His reference, then, is to a termination of married union—presumably associated with *some* form of legal divorce. If the unbeliever seeks this, then the believer is "not bound." What can this mean? It cannot mean "not bound to be together," for in this the Christian would have no choice. It can only mean not morally bound by the ties of a legally and socially terminated marriage. In other words, he or she is free to remarry.

Some commentators refer to this as "Pauline privilege," but this may be misleading. Paul is not giving new legal enactments, but trying to generalize Spirit-guided advice for a particular set of situations. He upholds the ideal, but (like God with Abraham) seeks to find the best option in nonideal circumstances.

Some, again, have argued that a divorced Christian should never remarry, and that such remarriages always remain adulterous. This is absurd. The whole point of the Mosaic Law regulating divorce was to ensure that the woman had the means to remarry. We have already seen how Paul's words, "let her remain unmarried," contradict both himself and Jesus if taken legalistically. In any case, how could she seek "reconciliation to her husband" if he had remarried? Jesus' abolition of the double standard would make this parallel to the supreme "abomination" of Deuteronomy.[57] Paul was advising *all* women against marriage in the Corinthian context,[58] though elsewhere he gives the opposite advice.[59] The whole attempt to take his words legalistically leads to confusion and contradiction. He simply did not mean them to be taken thus. In the end, the advisability of divorce in any circumstances must remain a matter of individual counseling. While there are general guidelines, a legalistic approach really misses the point.

All this, of course, refers to the church's attitude.

Obviously a society will have to lay down civil laws regulating divorce, and it is in society's interest not to make these too lax. In English law, for example, adultery, cruelty, and desertion are the traditional grounds; recently "irretrievable breakdown of marriage" has been added, to avoid the need to manufacture grounds where none of the three others really exist. As legal grounds, telling people what they *can* do, we have no objection to them. But the Christian concentrates not on what people *can* do, but what they *ought* to do. This cannot be legislated, for it will depend on circumstances, as we have seen. To accept the four above as adequate legal grounds for divorce is certainly not to say that divorce is always the best thing if one of them applies.

Divorce, therefore, is absolutely a last resort. God expects Christians to work together to preserve a marriage relationship. But he wants it to be a *genuine* marriage—not one which is so in outward form only. This, we remember, is irrespective of how the couple came to be married, or of whether or not they now feel that it was a mistake. Any two individuals, seeking close union in a fallen world, are going to have problems. If they do not, then they are either not real individuals or else have not understood what such a close union means. It is as well that a young couple recognize this at their wedding. The prince who gallops off with the beautiful maiden to "live happily ever after" is a mannequin, not a real person. But problems are overcome through being faced, not through being ignored. This is the first lesson to learn.

It would not be possible to write a manual on how to solve all marriage problems. For one thing, the variations on the kinds of problems are very large indeed—as large as the number of individual personalities in the world. For another thing, it is often a matter of judgment and counseling to decide which of two situations applies. Thus, in a marriage the husband might feel that his wife was not subject, while the wife felt her husband too authoritarian. Nevertheless, it might be useful to outline a few basic kinds of problem. Each of them is really based on some misunderstanding of a biblical teaching on marriage already noted in this book.

First, there may be a failure to realize the basis of marriage. A marriage is based on mutual commitment. Its validity does not depend on feelings, nor on the method of selection of a partner (for example, whether it was a mistake). Some people have never really accepted the fact that they *are* married (for better or worse), and had better stop complaining and get on with trying to make it work.

Second, there may be a failure to *"leave"* father and mother. A girl who runs home to mom after any quarrel has not understood "leaving." A man who is still dominated by mother or father has not understood it either. A son or daughter is always responsible to see that parents are cared for,[60] but is not required to "obey" after marriage. Moreover, the *first* commitment should thenceforth be to the marriage partner, and his or her welfare should come first.

Third, there may be a failure to *"cleave"* together. This means that they regard themselves as one unit socially and financially. They should be open with one another, having no secrets. They should be closer to each other than to anyone else. If formerly they have had a close friend of the same sex, this friendship must now consciously be relegated to second place in their commitments.

Fourth, they may not realize the "one-flesh" ideal. This involves several things. It means that the other person's body is regarded as a part of one's own. There is, therefore, no reason to have any shame in each other's naked presence.[61] But it also means that they should cherish and care for the partner's body *as though it were their own*.[62] This initially may be an attitude to take up, though it should become also a feeling which comes automatically.

Fifth, and connected with this, they may fail to have regular sexual intercourse. This is a clear biblical command, and unless there are very pressing reasons (or the marriage is already in shreds for other reasons), all Christian couples should follow it.

Sixth, they may fail to recognize God's order for the directing of the unit. The husband is to be the head *as Christ is head of the church*. This means that he leads by example, but also that he has the institutional authority and responsibility for any decisions. He will listen to his wife, and in love may sacrifice himself for her or follow her advice against his own inclination. But the responsibility is in the end his to make policy decisions. The wife is to be fully an individual with ideas of her own, but (except in extreme circumstances) is to be "subject" where these go against a decision of her husband's. Approached positively by both sides, this is a recipe for a good relationship. Not understood, it can lead to constant bickering.

Seventh, they may fail to recognize the importance of family life. They are a one-family unit within the wider family of the church. But this means spending time together *as a family*. Sometimes couples too busy in church work neglect each other and drift apart. Certainly disciples of Jesus are supposed to love him more than any earthly ties.[63] But Paul recognized that in a normal, healthy Christian marriage, one would have divided interests in a way a single person would not.[64] In many circumstances, the power of a husband-wife team (such as Aquila and Priscilla) can be greater even than the individuals singly, for they are an encouragement to each other. But for this to happen they need either to be in the same work, or at least to fully understand and sympathize with each other's work. In any case, they will still need to spend time together as a family; otherwise the relationship will suffer.

Eighth, they may fail to adjust to the coming of children. Both husband and wife should be equally involved and interested in the child's upbringing. The child is the fruits of *their* love, and there should be no lessening of their love for each other through transference of affection to the child. The child will be more emotionally secure and feel more loved if the parents make a conscious effort to work at pleasing and loving each other after the child is born. This they should do—however exhausting they find parenthood! They must also understand and agree on the biblical principles for bringing up children. Disagreement over punishment, etc. can cause severe problems. If they really cannot agree, then it would be best to seek spiritual counseling.

Last, they must be faithful in thought and deed. This is helped, of course, if they both are "anxious to please" their partners in dress, appearance, and sexual enjoyment. Romance and attraction may be based on feelings, but they can also be worked at. But, in any case, both should be faithful. This may be especially hard to do *in thought,* but this is what Jesus required. Prayer is the answer to temptation.

One final word of caution. We have outlined some of the misunderstandings of the Christian teaching on marriage. Remember, it may be unhelpful of a man or woman who thinks that his or her partner's understanding is deficient to aggressively brandish the teaching over that partner. A gentle reeducation may help to heal, but an aggressive attempt to instantly enlighten is more likely to cause even more problems.

CHAPTER TWELVE

The Single Person

Readings: Genesis 2:18-24
  Matthew 19:10-12
  1 Corinthians 7:17

In speaking of the single person, we should remember that there are several distinct groups which fall under that general title. It may be useful to categorize them here:

(1) Those who remain single because they view the celibate life as a higher calling;
(2) those who are single because they have not yet reached the usual age for marriage in their communities, but who have every prospect of marriage;
(3) those (for example, missionaries) who have never married because the conditions in which they work are too difficult to provide properly for a family;
(4) those who have never found anyone with whom they could enter the commitment of marriage, and are now likely to remain single;
(5) the widowed or divorced.

Throughout history many have praised the celibate life, but the idea is against scriptural teaching. God himself said, "It is not good for man to be alone." Also, marriage is a higher calling insofar as the "one-flesh" relationship reflects better the image of the Triune God. Neither the Bible nor Jewish thinking prized celibacy in itself. No unmarried man, for example, could sit on a Jewish council.[1] Since Paul had apparently done so, he was probably a widower at the time of his ministry, and he insisted on the right of apostles to be married.[2] Peter was also married.[3] The only passage which could be cited to advocate perpetual virginity is based on a misunderstanding, as we shall see.[4] The idea is sectarian or pagan.

The other four categories are all those in which a Christian may find himself or herself. They are, of course, blurred categories, for marriage can come to even the most apparently confirmed bachelor or spinster. But it is still useful to distinguish them.

To the person waiting for the right partner, the Bible says little that is specific. Generally it will be a time during which he (or she) is developing and maturing as a person, especially in the spiritual dimension. In actual fact, the kind of general characteristics which should be forming in a Christian are themselves very good preparation for marriage. The kind of close relationships which should be forming with other Christians are also good preparation for the closer ones of marriage. Thus, Paul entreats us "to lead a life worthy of the calling to which you have been called, with all lowliness and meekness, with patience, forbearing one another in love, eager to maintain the unity of the Spirit in the bond of peace."[5]

But there are a couple of more specific aspects. One is that the individual should be finding his or her identity as a person. The church is to show the "manifold wisdom of God,"[6] but it is not always easy to steer between a boring conformity to stereotype and a rejection of valid universals of Christian manhood or womanhood. To be masculine or feminine will mean something in any society. A person should strive to be that something *without* becoming a mannequin. To most of us, masculinity implies strength, but emotion and tenderness are clearly marks of biblical men after God's own heart. To most of us, femininity implies softness and dependence, but the "good wife" of Proverbs 31 is also independently resourceful. A girl should be feminine, a boy masculine, but without losing balance as a person.

Similarly, it is right and good for a boy or girl to dress and act in a way attractive to the opposite sex. But this should stop short of being sexy for the sake of being sexy. Those who are deliberately sexy are encouraging others to see them as sex objects rather than as people. This is bad, both because it could incite lust and because it would be no basis on which to begin a relationship. Thus far, preparation for marriage runs along the same lines as becoming a mature and balanced man or woman. But there is one other factor. Paul implies that the husband should rightly be concerned to please his wife and the wife her husband. This means that one will have to find out something about the ways in which (in that society) men and women tend to react and think differently.

As we turn to the third category of single person, we might look at Paul's words to the Corinthians. They were given not as Christian doctrine, but as a piece of personal advice "in view of the impending distress."[7] Violent opposition to the gospel from some Jewish factions was springing up everywhere. Nero was emperor. The church was in the birth pangs of a new age.[8] Paul's view of marriage was a very high one. He could not imagine a proper marriage except where husband and wife had constant care for each other's well-being and happiness.[9] Therefore, he said, his personal advice would be that it was better to remain single than have the pains and cares of so close a love-bond in times of difficulties. But he was not lauding celibacy. He was giving practical advice in a particular situation, just as in practical advice for a different situation to Timothy some years later, Paul said that his personal preference was for younger widows to remarry and have families.[10] There is no contradiction here, but differing advice in differing circumstances.

Today there may be circumstances where Christians are being mercilessly persecuted, and many would be better off without the cares of family attachments to add to their troubles. There may be other circumstances where the difficulties of mission work would make a single person more suitable for the task than a married person with a family. It is not good for man (or woman) to be alone, but we do not live in an ideal world. Many good things have to be sacrificed by those warriors of the faith willing to work in such circumstances; family may be one of them. Jesus himself, because of his task, had to sacrifice the completeness a man was intended to find in marriage, along with the closeness of other family ties.[11] On a spiritual level, Christ's masculinity is to be united with the femininity of his bride, the church. Yet, on a purely human level his sacrifice of normal, fulfilling family relationships was a permanent loss, a necessary price to pay. Paul, like Jesus, sacrificed the joy he would have found in a wife, rejoicing to be "filling up" the afflictions necessary to the welfare of the church.[12] Some Christians today, with special tasks, may be called upon to make this sacrifice. This comes from a calling of God.[13]

The fourth category contains those who, for all kinds of reasons, simply never found anyone with whom they could share their lives. Some, of course, may have some serious mental or physical handicap which has deterred marriage. But there is a large group of Christians who, realizing the permanent nature of the marriage commitment and the seriousness with which the Christian enters it, have never found anyone with whom they felt they could enter so final a commitment. When Jesus made it clear to his disciples that marriage was permanent for a Christian, their reaction was, "If this is the situation between a husband and wife, it is better not to marry." Jesus replied that some remain unmarried because of some physical disability from birth or later human action, while others remain unmarried because of the kingdom of Heaven.[14] In its context the primary meaning of this is not, as is often supposed, that they give up marriage to serve God. It means rather that because they are Christians, they have a high view of marriage as a permanent commitment; and so they feel it better to forego marriage than to marry and make a mess of it. An unmarried person may be more use to the kingdom than a married one who feels bound by a relationship which is unhappy. Viewed positively, this could mean that something of value (marriage) is sacrificed because *for that individual* this is best.

The last category is that of the divorced or widowed. The Bible makes it clear that the death of a spouse fully releases a partner from the marriage bond,[15] and he or she should be encouraged to remarry.[16] Marriage ties are to be transcended in Heaven; so no problems will arise.[17]

The last three categories mentioned can all mean that a person spends a single life. Some books speak of "God making it up" to such a person. But we should be careful. When God said, "It is not good for man to be alone," he was aware that Adam already had a full spiritual capacity. Apparently, though, God did not think that any companionship with himself could effectively fill the human lack. Nor did he feel that it could be filled by any animal. There is a definite need for a certain kind of human link, and this is filled neither by a spiritual life, nor by keeping a cat or a parrot. Yet, to some extent the need meant to be filled in marriage can and should be filled by other human relationships. For a time Ruth cleaved to Naomi.[18] Her words, "Where you go I will go, and where you stay I will stay. Your people will be my people . . . etc." imply a kind of commitment met at a deeper level in marriage. A close companion with whom to share (whether a relative or a close friend) can help to fulfill the human need. The relationships within the church can also do this. A working relationship in some worthy cause can also do it. Paul, though apparently without a wife, seldom traveled alone.[19] Something of the kind of "helper" experience in marriage can be met at a different level in such close relationships with co-workers. There may, of course, be dangers, especially if the co-worker is a member of the opposite sex whom one finds attractive. But it can be a valid way of meeting the lack, and could meet it much better than an unhappy marriage would.

The sexual needs which are met in marriage, of course, cannot really be met in any other way. There is no real substitute for regular sexual expression within a loving relationship. That is why Paul says it is better to *marry* than to burn.[20] The Bible is silent on all the other alternatives which may be suggested (for example, special prayer, plenty of exercise and cold showers, masturbation, or reliance on natural release for a man during sleep). We can give, then, no rigid advice, and the individual will have to work it out in a personal way with God.

There are other possible losses through remaining in a single state—such as the loss of an extended family, or lack of contact with children. Again it can be a good thing to find some substitutes for these. The church should be a kind of extended family, and there may also be opportunities for work with children within it. We may know of instances where bachelors or spinsters have identified too strongly with their Christian work. Yet, approached rightly, they can bring a dedication (without harmful possessiveness) beyond that of others. The key is that the fulfillment of their own emotional needs should be incidental, and their focus remain on the needs of those with whom they work.

It is, then, "not good for man to be alone." Yet, in our world today there are many other things which are not good, and this is only one of them. For some people, the unmarried state could be the best thing. The secret above all is contentment. We should learn, like Paul, whatever state we are in, to be content.[21] This does not stop us from seeking ways to make good any emotional lack which we may have in our lives, but it means that our peace of mind and heart are fundamentally based on Jesus.[22]

APPENDIX 1

Homosexual Relationships

The traditional opposition of the church to homosexuality has recently been loudly challenged by various groups, individuals, and publications claiming compatibility between Christian faith and homosexual activity in "committed relationships." The arguments they use are generally similar, and in the present comments we will restrict references to two typical publications. One is a statement of the view of the Gay Christian Movement, and the other bears names well-known in Christian circles.[1]

We will not here be concerned with popular misconceptions about homosexuals, the controversy over what causes homosexual tendencies, or the effectiveness of psychological therapy to "cure" them. Rather, we shall seek to examine the basic moral issues from a Christian standpoint. Can homosexual relationships ever be an acceptable life-style?

To begin with, it would be useful to point out that the argument is often based on a confusion of terms. The dictionary definition of "homosexual" is: "having a sexual propensity for persons of one's own sex" (i.e., whether male or female). But in practice the word is often used in three distinct senses:

(1) someone who enjoys the society of his (or her) own sex;
(2) someone who is physically attracted toward those of his (or her) own sex;
(3) someone who "lusts" for or actually engages in sexual acts with those of his (or her) own sex.

Sexual attraction is not lust, for lust involves a *mental* consummation of the sex act.[2] To emphasize the distinction between the three above situations, we might make an analogy. Who would wish to confuse: (1) a man's enjoyment of his sister-in-law's company, (2) his finding her sexually attractive, and (3) his having sex with her? Attraction to someone with whom sexual acts would be wrong can at strongest be called "temptation." This in itself is not sin, for Jesus was tempted *on all points* as we are, yet without sin.[3] Whatever, therefore, our view of homosexual *acts,* the temptation to commit them is not itself a sin.

But what *should* be our attitude toward sexual *acts* between those of the same sex? Are they *always* wrong, or are there circumstances in which they may be right? As Christians we must take our standards from Scripture.

Many people may expect us to begin from the story of Sodom's destruction, but in fact this is not altogether relevant here. The Sodomites (like the later Gibeonites[4]) were bent on committing what would have amounted to homosexual rape of visitors to their city.[5] Later, Jews saw their sins primarily as those of a lack of social care,[6] pride,[7] and a breach of hospitality to strangers.[8] The particular expression of this was indeed in fornication and lust.[9] But neither censure of homosexual rape, nor later condemnation of idolatrous male prostitution[10] need necessarily imply rejection of homosexual acts within caring relationships.

It would seem valid, however, to begin from an apparently plain Old Testament condemnation of *all* homosexual acts: "You shall not lie with a male as with a woman."[11] "Gay Christians" have approached this ban in two basic ways. One has been to suggest that it refers only to certain *kinds* of homosexual practice, perhaps anal intercourse or the forcible rape of the vanquished by their conqueror.[12] This is unconvincing, for the phrase used is a very general one meaning to "lie down with" and occurs over 100 times in the Old Testament. Its context is also perfectly general. To read into it something more specific and restricted amounts to forcing the text around to a personal view.

A second "gay" approach to this has been to suggest that it is to be regarded in the same light as, for example, some of the dietary laws of the Old Testament.[13] "In the New Covenant," they say, "has come a dawning realization that such laws and taboos are unnecessary." But this argument has major flaws. First, in both instances the ban on homosexual acts comes in a context of condemning the sins of previous inhabitants (for example, child sacrifice, incest, adultery, and sex relations with animals).[14] The ceremonial and dietary laws were never given in such a context, nor were the Canaanites censured for not keeping them. In other words, the ban on homosexual acts relates to issues of *universal morality*.

This may be confirmed by more fundamental considerations of biblical interpretation. In Genesis, God pronounced that all his created things were good;[15] and in the new beginning with Noah he said, "Everything that lives and moves will be food for you."[16] The later Mosaic prohibitions were not part of some original natural order laid down by God, but were often primarily (like, for example, circumcision itself) object lessons on holiness. When Jesus taught that *in themselves* foods could not defile, he was simply going back beyond the Mosaic Law to the more fundamental revelation of God's designs in Genesis.[17] Paul makes the connection even more explicit. He objects to those who order others "to abstain from certain foods, which God created to be received with thanksgiving.... For *everything God created is good, and nothing is to be rejected if it is received with thanksgiving.*"[18] The Mosaic dietary laws, given for a particular purpose to Israel, were not based on anything fundamental in God's stated design in Genesis. They are not, therefore, to be enforced in the New Covenant.

But it must be emphasized that the removal of Jewish restrictions in the New Covenant is not simply based on a principle of "anything goes." It is based on a return to what was fundamental in God's design, as stated in Genesis. When Jesus applied the same principle to sexual morality, the implications were quite different. The Mosaic divorce laws were a concession in an imperfect world, for "at the beginning the Creator made them male and female. 'For this reason a man will leave his father and mother and be united to his wife, and the two will become one flesh.' "[19] Jesus certainly did not suggest *relaxing* the Mosaic laws on this point. He did not suggest that "the only rule should be love," as have some modern theologians. He insisted that God's original design was for monogamous, heterosexual marriage, and that this establishes the right pattern for marital/sexual behavior. He was, of course, answering a question about divorce, not homosexuality; but it is interesting to note that his answer deliberately joined Genesis

1:27 and Genesis 2:24. God's creation of humankind as "male and female" is linked by Jesus to God's intention that the "one-flesh" union of man and wife should make up one complete human unit. It is difficult to see how a union of two males or two females could do this. A married couple are a complete human unit, a single person might be seen in a sense as incomplete, but a homosexual "marriage" can be only a monstrosity. Within the framework of monogamous, heterosexual marriage there is, of course, a tremendous scope for variety and human creativity. But it is hard to avoid the impression that Jesus took this framework as divinely laid down.

Paul, like Jesus, saw God's stated intentions in Genesis, rather than the Mosaic Law, as the most fundamental guidelines for marriage.[20] But while Jesus' recorded ministry was in a culture where open homosexual relationships were rare, Paul circulated widely in areas where they were common. Thus Paul is more explicit on the issue. "Gay Christians" have taken three basic attitudes to Paul's words. Some have simply dismissed them as cultural prejudice, an attitude clearly unacceptable to those of us who believe Scripture to be God's revelation. A second group has suggested that Paul intended his censures to apply only to *certain kinds* of homosexual acts and not to others. Paul's actual language, as we shall see, makes this implausible. But the third suggestion is more subtle. It is that "Paul thought that all homosexual acts were bound to be prostituting and idolatrous. It is unlikely that he knew any people whose identity as human beings was bound up with their (homo)sexual orientation...."[21]

We should question two things about this. First, there is the assumption that there are people whose "identity as human beings" is homosexual, or "persons whose 'nature' itself appears to be homosexual."[22] We need not doubt the testimony of psychologists that in some people heterosexual activity produces indifference or revulsion, while homosexual activity seems "natural." But Christians base neither morality nor human identity on human feelings. A person may feel it "natural" to have sex with his camel, lose his temper, or beat his wife, but that neither makes it *right* nor a part of his "human identity." To compare a homosexual tendency with, for example, left-handedness[23] begs the question; no one seriously takes left-handedness as a moral issue. Of course, we are all born with or grow up to have different tendencies, feelings, or inclinations; but we recognize that some of them would incline us to do things which are *wrong*. We then regard those who *act* on such feelings as unenlightened, sick, or committing sin. If, for example, someone is "by nature" greedy or cruel, we would not take this to imply that it was right for him to follow these inclinations. Of course a "natural inclination" may *sometimes* lead a person to do the right thing.[24] But only God's *words* to us are a sure guide to right and wrong.[25]

The Genesis story itself indicates this in portraying Adam's sin as disobedience of divinely revealed moral laws.[26] It also indicates that human identity is essentially bound up with *God's* design for us: "in the image of God created he him, male and female created he them."[27] To be truly human is to be as God designed us to be; this is not always apparent from our built-in inclinations, as we all well know. The question, then, is not whether Paul was conversant with particular psychological conditions in our fallen world, but rather whether God has revealed any moral issues in homosexual relationships. We may, moreover, doubt the naive assumption that Paul knew only of "prostituting and idolatrous" homosexuality. Paul was widely traveled and could quote Greek classics.[28] Various famous Greek classics discuss the spiritual and physical aspects of faithful homosexual love between consenting freeborn men,[29] and it would be incredible for Paul to never have come across unmarried homosexuals in a "caring relationship."

So what does Paul actually say? In Romans 1 he speaks of those men who "suppress the truth in unrighteousness," and goes on: "Therefore God gave them up to the lusts of their hearts to impurity . . . gave them up to dishonorable passions. Their females exchanged natural relations for unnatural, and the males likewise gave up natural relations with females and were consumed with passion for one another, males committing shameless acts with males. . . ."[30] Paul's censure here certainly falls on the homosexual *acts,* rather than the inclination, but what has he in mind? Various implausible attempts have been made to restrict his censure to certain *kinds* of homosexual acts. Some have argued that the words "exchanged" (verse 26) and "leaving" (verse 27, KJV) restrict Paul's meaning to those who were once heterosexual. But this is a literalism which ignores all context. It would be like taking verse 23 to refer only to those who *personally* changed from God to idolatry. Paul is not speaking of individuals' decline so much as of the effects on *society* of deifying Nature rather than worshiping God. Had, moreover, he really meant his censures to primarily refer to their marital infidelity, he would surely have used the terms *andrcs* (men or husbands) and *gunaikes* (women or wives) and not *arsenes* (males) and *theleiai* (females).

Other commentators have argued that his reference to "lusts" (verse 24) excludes loving homosexual relationships. This is equally misleading, for the word used *(epithumias)* is a general word for a deeply felt desire.[31] As such, the term would fit admirably the instance of a person "drawn to someone of the same sex for the sake of love."[32] It carries no necessary suggestion of either a passing fancy or a mere desire to experiment. Moreover, Paul's complaint is not that they were *unfaithful* to their homosexual lovers, but that they exchanged the "natural" relationship of female for male to one of female for female, etc. It is useful also to note in passing that his introduction of the idea via *female* homosexuality nullifies the suggestion that he thought only of prostitution or male rape as a sign of conquest, for neither applied to females. He had in mind homosexual acts of free consenting adults, pronouncing such acts wrong and unnatural.

It is sometimes suggested that Paul is here using the word "natural" in the sense developed by the Stoics. Stoicism maintained that it was right to live "according to nature,"[33] and so defined the right as the natural. But though some Stoics had a strong idea of God,[34] in general the system was pantheistic. There was no concept of a verbal revelation from God. So to base morality solely on Nature (i.e., the observable world) could only lead to the conclusion of Aurelius: *"Whatever* happens, happens rightly."[35] But Paul believed the created world to be in bondage to decay, groaning in travail, so he would hardly have based morality on observed Nature.[36] Our assurance as to what is right is founded rather on God's verbal revelation.[37]

So Paul begins with assumptions very different from those of the Stoics. His suggestion in Romans 1 is certainly not that they have paid *insufficient* attention to deducing morality from Nature; rather, he argues that they have *substituted* Nature for God.[38]

They have refused to acknowledge God and open a dialogue with him during which they might learn the ways to righteousness.[39] His reference to the unnaturalness of homosexual acts is not to say that this is the way in which we *know* them to be wrong; it is only to categorize the kind of sin they are. His use of the terms "male" and "female" may, indeed, refer to the fact that human sexuality is part of a wider pattern found in Nature. But our knowledge of God's design in this is not based merely on direct observation; it refers also back to his statement of intent for human nature in Genesis 1:27. We have already seen how Jesus linked this verse on "male and female" with the later one on God's design for marriage. To be unnatural implies to the Christian a departure from what *God intended* in Nature, not merely from Nature as now observed.

In spite of all attempts to place a restricted meaning on Paul's censures, he could hardly have found words to make them more general. Sadly, the modern gay movement itself reflects his words. They too begin from "nature" rather than from God and his revelation. Mankind was made "male and female" (Romans 1:27; Genesis 1:27); the image and glory of God (verse 23) was to be shown in a one-flesh, husband-wife union. But, though professing wisdom (verse 22), they have exchanged this for an enshrined image of corruptible man based on "nature" (verse 23), not revelation. This different image is based on observed deepset desires of the heart (verse 24); the fact that some are attracted only by their own sex is said to make their "true nature" homosexual. Thus, basing morality on the creature rather than the Creator (verse 25), God gives them up to put their desires into unclean acts. Knowing that the Levitical judgment of God prescribes the death penalty, they yet not only do the acts but consent to them as good (verse 32). God's truth is not merely violated, but "suppressed" (verse 18).

The other main reference by Paul to homosexual acts is in the word *arsenokoitas*.[40] The word is made up of two Greek words: *arsen* (male) and *koitas* (going to bed with), and put together they mean "going to bed with a male."[41] The Greek word *koitas* (like the English phrase) commonly implies a sex act.[42] This is, for example, implied when *arsen* and *koitas* are similarly joined in the Septuagint Old Testament.[43] How have "gay Christians" reacted to such an apparently clear condemnation of homosexual acts of all kinds? First the word is presented as being "uncertain" or "problematic,"[44] and the various translations of it are presented as "proof" of this. This is unconvincing. Neither the fact that no exact English equivalent exists for it, nor any idiosyncracies of different translators can alter the fact that the Greek word is simple, perfectly general, and unambiguous. But from this point the gay Christian argument goes on to suggest that "The original intent seems to have been to single out specific *kinds* of same-sex practice that were considered deplorable."[45] No serious proof is advanced for this, and on the basis of pure conjecture it is said that it "may refer to sodomites"[46] or "could refer to male prostitution."[47] But if the apostle of Christ deliberately chose a general word ("go to bed with a male"), then we are surely not at liberty to arbitrarily suggest some limited meaning for it.

Some, indeed, have tried to give a linguistic backing by citing Romans 13:13 to argue that *koitas* can mean "sexual excess."[48] But in Romans 13:13 the word is plural, and it is joined under the same verb with a word for "excesses." In itself, it by no means implies any excesses and unless good reasons can be given, we should take it in *arsenokoitas* in its simple and usual sense. It would apply to any and all forms of homosexual activity, and in using it Paul surely meant a general censure. One writer puts it: "Paul could have chosen more specific terms such as *paiderastes* ('lover of boys') or *paidothoros* ('corrupter of boys') or *arrenomanes* ('mad after males'). But he went for the most general word available."[49]

Another point from Paul's comments is worth noting. Christians have sometimes seemed to regard homosexual activity as some kind of supreme evil or ultimate decline, reacting in shock and revulsion bordering on hysteria. Paul has no such reaction. *Arsenokoitas* is placed alongside sins of fornication, lying, greed, covetousness, and extortion.[50] He regarded homosexual acts as wrong and unnatural, but not as some kind of supreme or special evil.

Nevertheless, if God's revelation implies that such acts *are* wrong, then for us to say so is not to be unloving, but simply to be true to what God has said. So how should we regard the homosexual? Again, we need to be careful about the different uses of this term. We have noted that to be attracted toward an act which would be wrong is temptation, not sin. Someone facing and resisting such temptation should receive all the compassion and help which fellow-Christians can give, and should never be afraid to seek confidential counseling in a spirit of love. If the problem persists, he may be advised to avoid situations of particular temptation.[51] But this is based on sense, not on some hysterial "branding" of him as a creature set apart. If he (or she) should fall into the temptation and then afterwards repent, what then? When the adulteress confessed Jesus as "Lord," the sinless Christ replied, "Neither do I condemn you; go, and do not sin again."[52] Homosexual activity is not a special sin, and God's forgiveness and cleansing are available.[53]

Today, however, there is another group besides the tempted and the repentant. There are those who openly and unrepentantly engage in homosexual acts, "gay Christians." We are in no position to judge their individual consciences before God, but since he ranks their acts with incest it would seem that we have guidance on how to react. They are not to be accepted in fellowship as Christians, but treated as though unconverted.[54] This does *not* mean that they are to be hated or reviled; Christians are to *love* all neighbors.[55] The protection of God's flock may at times call for firmness, but a gentle and loving spirit is essential. Homosexual activity is not a special sin, and those who unrepentantly continue in it seem no more deserving of *social* ostracism than the fornicator, adulterer, proud, or avaricious. Do those who express fear that the young may "catch" it also fear the contagious nature of heterosexual debauchery, pride, or avarice? Let us be unafraid to speak for the right, but let us also be consistent with *God's* standards.

One last point. This book has emphasized that neither right and wrong nor the validity of a marriage are based on feelings. A person whose feeling remains homosexually oriented may nonetheless validly get married. And if once Christians recognize that this is not a temptation set apart from others, we may see the time when, like other temptations, it may be shared with a prospective spouse in a spirit of mutual respect and affection.

POSTSCRIPT:

This postscript deals briefly with other kinds of sexual deviation:

Paederasty (intercourse with young boys) or the more general *paedophilia* (sexual attraction toward young children) are two such deviations. Paederasty is obviously one kind of homosexuality, but (in spite of popular myths) there seems to be no reason to expect homosexuals to have paedophilic tendencies any more than heterosexuals. Scripture makes no specific reference to paedophilia, but it is obvious that: (1) sexual acts in such cases cannot be within marriage; (2) they must therefore either be paederasty or fornication, either of which are wrong; (3) since they involve inducing *children* to participate in such wrong actions, they must come directly under the curse of Jesus.[56]

The *use of animals for sex* generally produces feelings of revulsion in our society, though in some cultures it is common. The Old Testament does forbid it,[57] ranking it with social injustice, etc.[58] But more fundamentally, God has said that there was no animal companion found suitable for man, and sex is properly a part of that companionship for which man and woman were made. An animal, unlike a child, cannot (properly speaking) be corrupted, but such acts are clearly wrong by God's standards.

The wearing of the clothes of the opposite sex *(transvestism)* is also forbidden in Scripture.[59] But the same passage forbids wearing linen and wool mixed, so its relevance today might be doubted. Again, however, there are more basic questions involved. Clothes are not, of course, *in themselves* male or female, but particular items are *seen* as for males or females in any society. So (as with any issue of symbolism) what is important is the *motivation* for wearing a particular garment. A unisex garment is not usually worn with any real idea of exchanging sexual roles. But a real transvestite wears particular clothes precisely because he (or she) *sees* them as female (or male). Transvestism is not, of course, to be identified with homosexuality, but it is hard not to see in it a comparable wish for exchange of gender role. This is unacceptable. It may not always be possible in practice to draw a clear line between, say, acceptable pantomime and unacceptable "drag artistry." It may not always be clear what *is* to be regarded as male or female clothing in times of change. But the principle itself is clear.

Other deviations such as *exhibitionism, voyeurism, fetishism, sadism,* and *masochism* could be mentioned. In each case, one may discern a departure from God's intentions for sex, and it is on this basis we pronounce them wrong.

In all this, however, we must remember that these are not special kinds of sin. The repentant deviant, or those tempted in this way, need our help, love, support, and compassion just as those tempted in any other way. The unrepentant is excluded from our fellowship, but not from our love.

APPENDIX 2

Paul on Dressing for Church

In Chapter 10 we argued that New Testament principles of church ministry are still applicable today. One passage which needs dealing with in this context is 1 Corinthians 11:3-16. All too often this passage is either "taken literally" or alternatively is casually dismissed. To do the former borders on Pharisaism, but to casually dismiss it brings a danger of basing our lives on our own feelings rather than God's revelation. What we need to do is to identify some basic principles of biblical interpretation and spiritual life.

Both Jesus and Paul distinguished inner spiritual realities from external forms.[1] The external forms are important only insofar as they symbolize something of inner realities *to those concerned*. Thus, to a person who associates idolatry with the eating of meat offered to idols, it would be wrong to eat such meat.[2] But it is also possible for a symbol to become some kind of fetish, having lost the connection in people's minds with some spiritual reality and so becoming an end in itself. Perhaps the best example of this is the brazen serpent. Originally ordained by

God, it later became a fetish.[3] In a sense, the Temple,[4] hand washing,[5] and various other things (for example circumcision) had a similar position in Jesus' day. Symbols are useful only if they point to spiritual realities; otherwise they become counterproductive.

Now if we take something like the New Testament pattern of ministry, it is not a question merely of external form and symbolism. A fundamental part of God's New Covenant prophecy was that his Spirit would be poured out on all people with resulting revelation and prophecy.[6] It is from this basic pattern of the New Covenant that Paul's teaching on spiritual gifts arises.[7] The form of meeting he then describes[8] is simply a natural expression of the Spirit-based ministry. If "to each is given the manifestation of the Spirit for the common good,"[9] then what can be more natural than simply to share the manifestations with one another? What can be more obvious than to include in this time of sharing a meal like the last supper, commemorating the Lord's death as he instructed?[10]

It must be emphasized that there is no way in which this can be seen as merely external detail, arising from cultural factors. Far from it. It cut totally across Corinthian and Hebrew culture. Sharing together in their ministry and love feasts were slaves and the city treasurer. Their fellowship transcended class barriers.[11] They had ex-idolaters and the ruler of the synagogue, thus transcending religious barriers.[12] There were men and women, in a culture where it was unthinkable for wives to eat with husbands.[13] Such a unique gathering relates to New Covenant truth, not to culture, for it is totally alien to culture.

On the other hand, Paul's comments on covering or uncovering of heads in 1 Corinthians 11 are in a different category. They do not relate in any obvious way to New Covenant principles, but to external symbolism, and they do clearly relate to Graeco-Jewish culture. A detailed exposition is available elsewhere on this, but a brief summary may be given here. Rabbinical sources show that to the Jews it was very improper for a woman to uncover her hair.[14] To uncover it was a symbol that she had been accused of adultery.[15] For a Jewess to uncover her hair when leading prayer would certainly "dishonor her head" (i.e., her husband).[16] It would be like a self-accusation of adultery, and she might as well cut off her hair altogether, as some commentators say was the sentence for adultery at that time.[17] On the other hand, for a Jewish man to cover his head while praying would only indicate (like the priest before God[18]) an unworthiness in God's presence. This would shame his head, Christ, whose work makes us worthy to enter God's presence.[19] There is, incidentally, no evidence that Jewish men normally wore prayer shawls at this time; the practice arose later.[20]

The situation for Greeks is less obvious. In public, respectable women often covered their hair with their *himation*,[21] though this may not have been universal. In any case, they had no cultural guidance as to what was proper in a mixed banquet of men and women, for such things were unheard of in Corinth.[22] Only *hetaerae* and flute-girls (both courtesans) attended male banquets.[23] Should the married women copy their "liberated" sisters, the *hetaerae*? Should they follow the Jewish women; or was this, like circumcision, a part of Jewish Law which need not apply to Gentiles? Paul was in no doubt. Prostitution (while a normal and accepted way of Greek life) cut quite across the Christian approach to sex and marriage. It would be far better to identify with the

Jewish symbolism, and its associated ideals of partnership in a truly liberated marriage. In this sense, the head covering became the woman's "authority."[24] She symbolically declared her liberated acceptance of a role as a Christian wife.[25] This enabled her without fear of being misunderstood to break with either the synagogue tradition of nonparticipation of women,[26] or with Corinthian tradition of only the harlots joining male company.

But in all this Paul's comments relate to a culturally based symbolism of head coverings. His statements are made on an "If ... then ..." basis.[27] In one Greek play, the reaction of a Corinthian common-law wife whose jealous husband cuts off her hair[28] bears out the point Paul makes. The apostle also refers to "custom"[29] in a way he never ever did over moral issues. All this, and the other strands of his argument, would become clearer in a detailed exposition, but this is not the place for it. Such exposition, however, can only lead to the conclusion that it would be impossible in a Western culture for head coverings to be a symbolic "authority" as they were then. The wedding ring performs that function for us, and in other societies other symbols may be the norm. What we must do, therefore, is to understand the spiritual essence of the teaching, and the purpose of the symbolism. We should not follow blindly, as some kind of fetish, an external form which means nothing to our society. It is the institution of marriage which we must stand by, even if (as in Paul's day) the Christian conception of it is so much higher and more liberated than contemporary pagans. If we take a stand on symbolism (for example, on wedding rings), it should be against those who reject the symbol because they reject the institution itself (as do perhaps some of the wilder elements of "women's lib"). Our liberation is different in kind from theirs.

We might also note Paul's other reference to similar issues in 1 Timothy 2:8-15. The context seems to be one of Christian gatherings, and again dress is touched upon. The Greek word *hōsautōs* which begins verse 9 usually means "in like manner" (as KJV), not merely "also" (as RSV and NIV). Some take this to mean that Paul expects women to pray in like manner to the men just mentioned. However, his main point is that in Christian meetings the women should be known for their good works, not for the extravagance of their dress. Modesty (not "shamefacedness," KJV) is called for. The women should also (as the next verses show) not usurp authority over the men. Paul is usually very conscious of the witness presented to outsiders.[30] He is also conscious of the fact that the position of the Christian wife is one of liberation and equality as a coheir open to the Spirit to minister through her. He is, therefore, all too aware of the need to avoid giving any wrong impression to the people around. Dress, because it symbolizes attitude, can do this. He speaks, of course, to that particular time and culture; he is not implying that men can never misuse dress. He also refers to a context of church gatherings; he does not expect a grey uniformity and a renouncement of all party clothes. But once we understand this, we see his point. Physical symbols reveal inner attitudes.

We emerge, therefore, with two firm convictions and commitments. The first is that God's revelation in the New Testament is relevant today on practical aspects of marital relationships and church order and ministry. It is not all to be written off as culturally based or out of date. But the second is that certain aspects of purely external symbolism do relate to particular cultures in that only in those contexts do they symbolize particular spiritual realities. They are nothing in themselves, and outside that context would become pointless fetishes. We should always, then, be seeking through the Spirit to understand the spiritual truths behind any revelation God made through his apostles. We are heirs, and God wants us to grow into mature sons and daughters.

APPENDIX 3

Women as Coheirs

How did the attitudes of Jesus and Paul toward women relate to the prevailing attitudes of their day? To consider this, we must first note the three elements of their background and culture. First, there was the influence of the intellectual heritage of Greece, the Hellenistic influence. Second, there was the all-pervading political influence of Rome, and its laws concerning women and family. Last, and obviously most important, there was the intensely religious, cultural, and legal traditions of the Hebrew nation into which both were born.

The Hellenistic cultural influence was dominated by the thinkers of Athens, among whom the general view was that woman was inferior. On this, for once, even those twin stars of philosophy, Plato and Aristotle, agreed.[1] The position of women in social life reflected this. One Greek well put it: "We have courtesans for the sake of pleasure, but concubines for the sake of daily habitation and wives for the purpose of having children legitimately, and of having a faithful guardian of all our household affairs."[2] Woman was a means to an end—a chattel, drudge, or sex object.

Wives were seldom educated, and would be seen neither as equals nor as companions in any real sense. For pleasure and companionship, a husband (if he could afford it) would turn to some kind of prostitute. At banquets, for example, men would not have their wives, but *hetaerae* ("friends") or *auletrides* ("flute-girls" and "guitar-girls"). There was no idea of companionship between man and wife in a deep and committed relationship. Moreover, any women of political influence in historic Greece were prostitutes or ex-prostitutes whose power originated in sex appeal.[3]

The soldier-farmers of early Rome had no slave economy, and they lacked the leisured classes of Athens. Their genius was in action rather than in thinking, and their emphasis on order and legal institutions helped them conquer and rule many nations. Originally the man had absolute power *(patria potestas)* over his wife and children, but by Jesus' day this was inoperative. Women could hold property (their dowry was repaid if their husband divorced them), and they could divorce their husbands if they so chose. Even so, no woman could hold political power in her own right (though she might scheme like Nero's mother), and the virtue traditionally admired was loyalty to one's husband. However, marriage in practice was not very highly regarded, and divorce and remarriage were common, often for financial or political reasons. There were, of course, many currents and counter-currents of thought around that time—from Augustus Caesar's strong laws against adultery to Ovid's exaltation of adulterous "love." Overall, however, the woman occupied a higher place in Roman than in Greek life. Yet still there was little real tradition of marriage as a committed relationship of companions.

WOMEN AS COHEIRS

The Hebrew tradition differs greatly from both Greek and Roman cultures. Nominally it began (as we trace in Scripture) with a patriarchal system. Yet, in actual fact at no stage of Hebrew history do women give the impression of being downtrodden serfs. At the start of the patriarchal period, Sarah generally seemed able to persuade Abram to do what she set her mind on.[4] When the nation was born, Miriam seems to have been a leading figure in her own right.[5] In the period of the judges, Deborah ruled with what seems to have been a forceful power of personality—nothing to do with sex appeal![6] In the times of the prophets, Hannah seems to be treated with great respect and tenderness by her husband, and her vow led to the birth of the great prophet Samuel.[7] The story of Ruth formed a background to the birth of the greatest line of Hebrew kings through her great-grandson David.[8] Later, the courage of the Jewish queen Esther saved her people, an event celebrated annually by the Hebrews in the feast of Purim.[9] None of this is patriarchalism. Moreover, the words of Genesis always stood before them. Woman was made to be a "help of man's like." She was an ally, a companion.

But what of the ideas which dominated rabbinical thinking in the days of Jesus and Paul? We must here be cautious about concluding too much. For one thing, the traditions were not actually written down until later. For another, in the to and fro of rabbinical discussion one can easily find selected quotations which give a slanted impression of the whole. Yet, taken as a whole, there does seem to be a marked movement from the Old Testament regard for women. Even Jewish apologist Claude Montefiore admitted, "No amount of apologetics can get over the implication of the daily blessing which Orthodox

Judaism has still lacked the courage to remove from its official prayer book: 'Blessed art thou, O Lord our God, who hast not made me a woman.' "[10] Women had to keep the prohibitions, but not the positive commandments of the Law.[11] They were seldom taught the Law, and one first-century Rabbi even said, "If a man gives his daughter knowledge of the Law, it is as though he taught her lechery."[12] In theory a woman could be called to read the Torah scroll in a synagogue, but in practice they were not because "of the honor of the congregation."[13] It was normal for Rabbis, like all Jewish men, to be married. Yet the Hillelite school, including Rabbi Gamaliel, the teacher of Paul,[14] regarded marriage lightly. Divorce could be for the most trivial of reasons—at, of course, the husband's wish and not at the wife's.[15] Moreover, keeping much female company, even of one's own wife, was deplored. "Talk not much with womankind," said one second-century Rabbi.[16] Later, propriety forbade a man to be alone with a woman (other than his wife),[17] to look at or greet one,[18] or even to speak with one on the street.[19] This was, of course, in contrast to the Greeks who preferred company of harlots to their own wives; this was an avoidance of female company altogether. The Jewish wife was certainly held in higher honor than the Greek wife, but neither Jews nor Greeks saw the wife as a suitable companion for study and scholarship. Standing outside the rabbinical tradition, the first-century Hellenistic Jewish philosopher Philo was equally depreciating of women: "It is suitable for women to stay indoors and to live in retirement."[20]

Now it is likely that the ordinary workingman (Jew or Greek) might differ in his practical treatment of his wife from the theoretical viewpoint of the scholars. But both Jesus and Paul were Rabbis.[21] Their craftsmen origins[22] would be quite normal in Rabbis, and this should not mislead us. Yet, if they were Rabbis, then how did they fit into the rabbinical tradition?

As we turn to look at the attitude of Jesus to women, we find an amazing thing. He stands as a unique figure. Not only does he smash through all the conventions for a Jewish Rabbi of his day, but he towers above most Christian men who have supposedly followed his example. In contrast with his perfect life, several attitudes often permeate our thinking. One is an attitude of condescension, patronizingly assigning to woman her "proper place." The implication behind this is usually that woman is in some way inferior—though it is usually cloaked in phrases like "man has been better fitted by God for certain tasks and woman for others." In practice this means that man can think, lead, and understand spiritual things, while woman makes the tea and arranges flowers. Needless to say, there is no biblical basis for this. God *commands* man to lead; he does not say that man is better fitted for it.

The second attitude often found is one which regards "female" things as somehow funny, irrational, and slightly amusing. Sadly, one often detects under this an inability to relate to a woman simply as a person. Some men find it hard to relate to women other than as sex objects (i.e., by flirting with them), or as a different species of child to be coddled and protected.[23] They can never take a woman seriously as, say, an intellectual or spiritual leader unless she is somewhat masculine.

A third approach, allied to this, is by those who are fearful of women and see their sexuality as a threat. Because fundamentally they see women as sex objects and not as people, they fear their own natural lusts and so thunder forth like Tertullian on the evils and dangers of the female sex. Some, admittedly, recognize that the problem is rather in themselves, but would still bar women from places of ministry.

Jesus had none of these approaches. He was one who, in the words of Dorothy Sayers, "never nagged at them, never flattered or coaxed or patronized; who never made sick jokes about them ... who rebuked without querulousness and praised without condescension; who took their questions and arguments seriously; who never mapped out their sphere for them, never urged them to be feminine or jeered at them for being female; who had no axe to grind and no uneasy male dignity to defend; who took them as he found them and was completely unselfconscious. There is no act, no sermon, no parable in the whole Gospel that borrows its pungency from female perversity; nobody could possibly guess from the words and deeds of Jesus that there was anything 'funny' about woman's nature."[24]

Fundamentally Jesus saw people as persons, each a disciple in his/her own right. Two incidents illustrate this. Some people would elevate motherhood as the supreme fulfillment of womanhood. One woman clearly had this idea and shouted, "Blessed is the womb that bore you, and the breasts that you sucked." But Jesus said, "Blessed rather are those who hear the word of God and keep it!"[25] Womanhood is no more exalted than manhood in procreation; but both are exalted in discipleship and as persons, without reference to sex. Jesus did not typecast woman as mother, or as domestic servant, as a second incident shows. When Martha asked Jesus to redirect Mary to a proper "womanly" role of serving the food, Jesus replied, "Martha, Martha, you are anxious and troubled about many things; one thing is needful. Mary has chosen the good portion, which shall not be taken away from her."[26] Jesus, in total opposition to the other Rabbis, encouraged Mary to receive spiritual teaching. Perhaps her later act[27] showed that she understood better than his male disciples. But fundamentally he related to her as a person; her sex was irrelevant.

This, in fact, marks off Jesus both from male chauvinists and from feminists. He saw no need to be either patronizingly patriarchal or touchily aggressive about femininity. He felt no need to make sweeping generalizations bolstered up by proof texts and "psychological insights." Women and men are simply individuals, and he enters their worlds and lives as such.

This is reflected first in his teaching. The illustrations of his parables often contain a male and a female example.[28] Likewise, in his references to the Old Testament he often referred to a woman and to men.[29] He often balanced his phrases such as, "father and mother,"[30] "brother and sister."[31] He referred to "publicans and harlots,"[32] the lowest profession for each.

A similar pattern emerges in his healings. He healed a son[33] and a daughter.[34] He healed a woman whose touch would have made him "unclean."[35] He even healed a mother-in-law—without even a nudge or a wink.[36] He singled out a crippled woman, calling her a "daughter of Abraham," to heal on the Sabbath.[37] He healed people because they were sick; their sex was irrelevant. He dealt with people according to their needs, not their sex. Thus, he accepted the woman with the ointment, seeing a repentant sinner where others saw only a sex object.[38] He forgave the adulteress (where was the adulter*er*?).[39] He praised the faith of the Syro-Phoenician woman,[40] and the giving of the poor widow.[41] He talked with the Samaritan woman at the well—to the amazement both of herself and of his disciples.[42] In fact, it was to her that he first stated his messiahship as he sought to convict her of sin and win her to faith.

Women usually seem to get the important news of Jesus first. His coming was first announced to Mary.[43] The first to broadcast his coming in Jerusalem was Anna.[44] The first to whom he proclaimed messiahship was the Samaritan woman.[45] The first to hear of his resurrection were women, and the first to see his resurrected body and touch him was Mary.[46]

Lastly, we note that he was willing to accept women as disciples in his band and to look to them as the providers for his needs.[47] He did not choose any to be apostles, but we would suggest that this was for reasons we have given in Chapter 10, and not because he thought them unfit. But in all respects he treated women simply and unembarrassedly as people.

Paul the apostle could not achieve the perfection of the sinless Jesus; yet his attitude too was remarkable. Brought up in the Hillelite tradition of Gamaliel,[48] Paul would normally have shared the rabbinical attitudes of his day. The Mishnah discouraged men from talking much with women, and its rules of propriety discouraged a man from being alone with a woman other than his wife.[49] The Talmud went further in discouraging even looking at or greeting married women, while it was disgraceful for a scholar to speak with a woman in the street.[50] Yet the Rabbi Paul at Philippi "sat down and began to speak to the women who gathered there."[51] One of these was a businesswoman, Lydia, not even a Jewess, but a Gentile "worshiper of God."[52] When she became a Christian she appealed to Paul, "If you consider me a believer in the Lord, come and stay at my house."[53] Paul had to choose. His rabbinical background would have led him to regard her firstly as a woman, and only secondarily as a disciple. He would have wanted to keep himself away from female company and would fear any gossip. On the other hand, her words had urged him to treat her as Jesus treated women—firstly as disciples and secondarily as women. The Rabbi Paul passed the test; he went to stay with her household.[54] In fact, her house, like quite a few other houses belonging to women,[55] became a standard Christian meeting place.[56]

This is all in harmony with Paul's general attitude to women. For example, his longest letter was apparently carried by a woman[57] and contains greetings to seven women by name.[58] He commends the work done by women, and regards them as "fellow-workers."[59] One woman he even calls his "patroness."[60] None of this conflicts with Paul's view of the husband as the head of the wife. Those who suggest a conflict generally misunderstand in several ways the meaning of headship. First, they mistake subjection for servility. Jewett,[61] for example, sees headship-subjection as comparable to a general-private relationship in an army. But if we wish to use a military analogy, the woman is the ally of the man, not an inferior rank. Between allies there may be one commander-in-chief, otherwise there would be chaos; but there is always consultation. The husband's headship implies an authority like that of commander-in-chief among consulting allies, and this is God's recipe to avoid chaos and disharmony. Jewett's alternative—"When mutual agreement cannot be achieved, the husband's preference should be honored by the wife in some instances, and the wife's by the husband in other instances"[62]—is vague and unrealistic. Who decides which instances are which?

Should they, like Roman Consuls Varro and Paulus, take command on alternate days? That arrangement led to the biggest defeat in Roman history. To have a clear commander-in-chief is better. Moreover, a commander-in-chief of allies implies no superiority. For example, the Greek commander-in-chief Agamemnon was neither a better man nor a better soldier than Achilles, his ally. In some cases, the husband is intellectually and spiritually inferior to his wife. But God has chosen to give a simple, unambiguous recipe to ensure order and harmony rather than chaos; and where God commands, God enables.

But this kind of military analogy omits a third vital point about Paul on the headship-subjection bond. The husband is to *love his wife as Christ loved the church.* He is to treat his wife as part of a one-flesh, one-body unity with himself. He is *head* of *one body,* not ruler of a vassal. Love, as Paul said, "does not insist on its own way."[63]

Lastly, we might note how misleading is Jewett's comparison of Paul's instructions on marriage with those to slaves to obey their masters.[64] Paul nowhere shows a concern to preserve the institution of slavery (which, unlike marriage, was never ordained by God). His instruction to slaves is concerned rather for their own spiritual growth, that they should be upright and trustworthy rather than scheming hypocrites.[65] His instruction to obey masters in this context was entirely right. But he himself recognized that freedom was preferable if obtainable.[66] Moreover, his instruction to Philemon to regard a slave as a brother was far more revolutionary (in its implication of a regard for the best welfare of that slave as an individual) than mere abolitionism.[67] Paul's instructions to slaves were entirely right for a situation where the institution was unalterably upheld by the might of pagan Rome.

But to compare this with marriage is absurd. Roman law set strict limitations on the actions of slaves, but gave little restriction to the private behavior of wives and husbands within their marriage. The husband-wife relationship was formed within the framework of a divinely ordained institution; and Paul's vision of headship-subjection was for a marriage where the very highest standards of Christlike love already operated.[68] Thus, while the instructions to slaves may be particular to a social context which no longer exists, those on marriage certainly are not.

No one should ascribe to Paul the perfection of Christ. His personal advice could be couched in terms colored by "masculine" thinking.[69] Yet we believe that fundamentally he broke with the rabbinical tradition in following his Lord's attitude to women. They are seen first as disciples and individual persons, and only secondarily as females.

The Christian leaders of the postapostolic age often abysmally failed to follow the lead of Jesus. This is not the place to enter into it, though there does seem to be evidence that those of the Reformed tradition tended to be particularly misogynist, while those in the tradition of Wesley, Finney, William Booth, Hudson Taylor, etc. accepted women fully as co-workers.[70] This could perhaps make us wonder whether a Christlike passion to reach and win individuals leads naturally to a view of women as individuals and potential co-workers. In any event, we would perhaps all do well to meditate long on the shining example of Jesus and the way in which his life and approach to men-women relationships shattered the traditions of his times.

Notes

Prologue
1. 2 Tim. 3:1-5.
2. 2 Tim. 3:16, 17.
3. Gen. 16:3, 4.
4. Gen. 29:21-28.
5. 1 Sam. 1:2.
6. 1 Sam. 25:43.
7. An implication from Mark 10:11.
8. Gen. 21:10, 12.
9. Josh. 8:2.
10. Hos. 1:2.
11. Matt. 19:4, 5; Mark 10:6, 7.
12. Matt. 19:8; Mark 10:5.
13. Matt. 19:8.
14. See Chapter 11 of this book.

Chapter 1
1. John 1:1, 2, 3, 14.
2. John 8:49, 54.
3. John 20:17.
4. John 13:31, 32.
5. Heb. 1:8.
6. 1 Cor. 15:28; Rev. 22:3.
7. 1 John 4:8, 16; 1 Cor. 15:28.
8. John 1:3; Col. 1:16.
9. Gen. 1:2.
10. Gen. 1:26.

NOTES

11. Gen. 1:27.
12. Gen. 1:28; 2:16, 17.
13. Gen. 2:19, 20.
14. Gen. 2:23.
15. Gen. 3:7.
16. Gen. 3:8.
17. Gen. 4:5.
18. Gen. 3:15.
19. Gen. 1:28.
20. Gen. 3:17-19 (a literal rendering).
21. See God's words in Gen. 21:12.
22. Prov. 31:16; Ruth 2:3.
23. The LXX rendering of it as "groanings" is adopted since the usual modern rendering of the Hebrew has no obvious sense and would be an odd phrase to use.
24. Gen. 3:16 (literal).
25. The Hebrew word translated "painful labor" is used to man and to woman (LXX has *lupē* in both).
26. Used only in Gen. 3:16; 4:7; Song 7:10. (LXX uses "turning.")
27. See, e.g., "rule" in Isa. 19:4; Dan. 11:3.
28. See Chapter 7.
29. Gen. 3:15 (literal).
30. We may take this as Paul (Gal. 3:16) takes the later word to Abraham.
31. Matt. 12:34; 23:33.
32. Gen. 3:15, last two clauses.
33. 1 Tim. 2:15.
34. 1 Cor. 15:22, 45.
35. Rom. 16:20, but note the active agent.
36. Matt. 19:19.
37. Gen. 2:7.
38. Gen. 2:7; 6:17; 7:15.
39. Gen. 2:7; also see 1:21, 24 (creature = soul).
40. Rom. 7:9; Gen. 2:17.
41. John 3:6.
42. 1 Cor. 15:45.
43. 1 Cor. 9:27; cf. Phil. 3:19; see also Acts 2:17; John 1:14; 1 Tim. 3:16.
44. Rom. 12:1; 1 Cor. 6:19, 20.
45. Rom. 8:14; Gal. 5:18.
46. Rom. 8:6; Col. 3:1, 2.
47. 2 Cor. 5:16.
48. Acts 2:47.

Chapter 2
1. John 8:49, 54; 13:31, 32.
2. Gen. 1:26, 27.
3. Gen. 2:18.
4. See Note 13.
5. Gen. 2:24.
6. Ruth 1:14.
7. Ruth 1:16, 17.
8. 1 Cor. 6:15, 16.
9. Eph. 5:25-31.
10. Gen. 3:7.
11. E.g., Isa. 1:21; Jer. 3, especially v. 20; Ezek. 23, especially v. 5; Hos. 2:16-19; 4:10.
12. Jer. 3:11-13; Hos. 2:19, 20.
13. *Of God:* Ex. 18:4; Deut. 33:7, 26, 29; Ps. 20:2; 33:20; 70:5; 89:19; 115:9-11; 121:1, 2; 124:8; 146:5; Hos. 13:9. *Of allies:* Isa. 30:5; Ezek. 12:14; Dan. 11:34.
14. John 13:13, 14.
15. Eph. 5:33.
16. E.g., Ex. 22:17.
17. 1 Cor. 7:36-38.
18. 1 Cor. 7:39.
19. Eph. 5:25; Tit. 2:4.
20. Tit. 2:4.

Chapter 3
1. Gen. 29:20.
2. Ex. 2:16-22.
3. 1 Sam. 18:20.
4. Gen. 26:34, 35; Judg. 15, 16.
5. Gen. 24; 28; 1 Kings 11:1, 8; Judg. 15, 16; 1 Kings 16:31.
6. 2 Cor. 6:14-16; 1 Cor. 7:39.
7. 1 Cor. 7.
8. Rom. 1:1; Tit. 1:1; Jas. 1:1; 2 Pet. 1:1; Jude 1; Rev. 1:1 (servant = slave, Greek *doulos*).
9. Rom. 8:15-17.
10. John 15:16.
11. 1 Chron. 17:1-12.
12. 1 Cor. 3:9.
13. 1 Thess. 5:26; Rom. 16:16.
14. 2 Cor. 5:15, 16.
15. 1 Cor. 10:24; Phil. 2:4.
16. Matt. 19:19; Luke 6:31.

Chapter 4
1. Gen. 34:12; Ex. 22:17; 1 Sam. 18:25.
2. Mishnah Kiddushin i:1; see also secondary sources: Alfred Edersheim, *Sketches of Jewish Life* (Grand Rapids, Mich.: Eerdmans, 1974); Joachim Jeremias, *Jerusalem in the Time of Jesus* (London: SCM Press, 1973; Philadelphia: Fortress, 1977); K. E. Keith, *The Social Life of a Jew in the Time of Christ* (London: The Church's Mission to the Jews, 1959).
3. Matt. 1:18, 20.
4. Gen. 24:67; John 2:1-11.
5. Matt. 19:6; Mark 10:9.
6. 1 Cor. 7:10; see Chapter 11 of this book.
7. Matt. 19:8; Mark 10:5.
8. Matt. 19:9.
9. Deut. 22:25-27.
10. Ex. 22:16, 17; Deut. 22:28, 29.
11. John 8:1-11.
12. Matt. 15:19.
13. Matt. 15:19.
14. Ex. 22:16, 17.
15. Rom. 14:15.
16. 1 Cor. 7:9.

Chapter 5
1. Stephen Cotgrove, *The Science of Society* (England: Allen & Unwin, 1972; U.S. edition 1978), n.p.
2. Gen. 2:18.
3. Gen. 4:1; Hebrew *yada* is normal word for "know."
4. Heb. 13:4, KJV.
5. Song 2:6; 8:3.
6. Song 7:8.
7. Prov. 5:18, 19.
8. Song 2:5; 5:8.
9. Gen. 26:8.
10. 1 Cor. 7:5.
11. 1 Cor. 7:4; Song 2:16; 6:3; 7:10, 12.
12. 1 Cor. 7:3, 33, 34.
13. 1 Cor. 7:5.
14. Lev. 18:19, 26; 20:18, 23; Ezek. 22:10.
15. Eph. 5:28-31.
16. Song 4:11.
17. Tim and Beverly LaHaye, *The Act of Marriage* (Grand Rapids, Mich.: Zondervan, 1976), p. 276.

18. Rom. 14:23.
19. We recommend Tim and Beverly LaHaye's *The Act of Marriage* (Zondervan, 1976), but choosing cookery books is more a matter of personal taste.
20. 1 Tim. 5:23.
21. Matt. 4:7.
22. Gen. 38:8-10.
23. Deut. 25:5-10.
24. 1 Cor. 7:5.
25. See Colin Brown, ed., *The New International Dictionary of New Testament Theology*, Vols. 1-3 (Exeter, England: Paternoster, 1975-1978; Grand Rapids, Mich.: Zondervan, n.d.), 1:499; G. Kittel and G. Friedrich, *Theological Dictionary of the New Testament*, Vols. 1-10 (London: SCM Press; Grand Rapids, Mich.: Eerdmans, 1964-1977), 5:587.
26. Deut. 23:17; Matt. 15:19; Acts 21:25; Rom. 1:29; 2:25; 1 Cor. 5:1; 6:18; Rev. 2:14.
27. 1 Cor. 6:15-17.
28. See Brown, *The New International Dictionary of New Testament Theology*, 2:582; Kittell, *Theological Dictionary of the New Testament*, 4:730.
29. Ex. 20:14; Lev. 20:10; Deut. 5:18; Jer. 13:27; Hos. 4:2.
30. John 3:17; 12:47.
31. John 8:11.
32. Matt. 15:19; Mark 7:21; 10:19; Luke 18:11, 20; see also Rom. 13:9; 1 Cor. 6:9; Gal. 5:19; Heb. 13:4.
33. Matt. 5:28.
34. Matt. 19:9.

Chapter 6
1. Matt. 5:28.
2. Col. 3:8.
3. Eph. 5:4.
4. Phil. 4:8.
5. E.g., Gal. 5:19. (*Akatharsia* is a very general word, including ritual and moral uncleanness; see Brown, *The New International Dictionary of New Testament Theology*, 3:102; Kittel, *Theological Dictionary of the New Testament*, 3:427; H. G. Liddell and R. Scott, *A Greek-English Lexicon* (London: Oxford, 1901; New York: Oxford, 1940), 1:46.
6. Gen. 38:8-11.
7. 1 Cor. 6:9, KJV; the term is analyzed in Appendix 1.

NOTES

8. E.g., the LaHayes in *The Act of Marriage* totally reject it; H. J. Miles in *Sexual Understanding Before Marriage* accepts it in some circumstances; John White in *Eros Defiled* says it isn't necessarily sin, but offers help for "deliverance."
9. Rom. 1:26; see Appendix 1.
10. Matt. 19:12; 1 Cor. 7:26, 32.
11. See Strabo, viii:378; Dion Chrysost. 37:34; Horace *Ep*, i:17, 36; Athenaeus, xiii:573.
12. 1 Cor. 6:15-20.
13. 1 Cor. 7:2, 9.
14. 1 Tim. 4:2.
15. Rom. 13:9, 10; Matt. 22:37-40.

Chapter 7
1. Eph. 5:21-24.
2. See Brown, *The New International Dictionary of New Testament Theology*, 2:156; Kittel, *Theological Dictionary of the New Testament*, 3:673.
3. 1 Cor. 12:26.
4. 1 Cor. 11:3.
5. John 5:18; Phil. 2:6.
6. Rom. 8:29.
7. Heb. 2:11.
8. Gen. 2:18.
9. 1 Tim. 3:4.
10. 1 Tim. 5:14.
11. From *hupo* (= under) *tasso* (= set in order). *Tasso* originated as a military term in the Greek citizen armies; see Brown, *The New International Dictionary of New Testament Theology*, 1:476; Kittel, *Theological Dictionary of the New Testament*, 8:27; Liddell, *A Greek-English Lexicon*, has *tasso* on 2:1759 and *hupotasso* on 2:1897.
12. Eph. 6:1; Col. 3:20.
13. 1 Pet. 3:6.
14. Eph. 5:25.
15. 1 Cor. 12:26.
16. John 15:15.
17. Eph. 5:28-31.
18. Rom. 13:1; 1 Cor. 16:16; 1 Pet. 2:13; 5:5.
19. Luke 2:51; 1 Tim. 3:4; Tit. 2:9; 1 Pet. 2:18.
20. Eph. 5:21.
21. Compare Eph. 5:21, 22; 1 Pet. 3:1; 5:5 (literal translation).

22. Luke 2:51; 1 Cor. 15:28.
23. Eph. 5:33.
24. Judg. 4:4ff.
25. 2 Kings 22:14.
26. 1 Sam. 25.
27. Plato—e.g., *Laws*, 781; Aristotle—e.g., *Politics*, 1:5.
28. 1 Pet. 3:7.
29. 1 Sam. 21:5; 1 Thess. 4:4.
30. 2 Cor. 12:9.
31. See Brown, *The New International Dictionary of New Testament Theology*, 1:193, 197; Kittel, *Theological Dictionary of the New Testament*, 6:700; Liddell, *A Greek-English Lexicon*, 2:1482.
32. 1 Pet. 2:21-23.
33. 1 Pet. 3:1.
34. Acts 5:29.
35. 1 Cor. 7:12-16.
36. 1 Cor. 7:39; 2 Cor. 6:14.
37. Matt. 19:8ff.

Chapter 8
1. 1 Tim. 5:14.
2. Germaine Greer, *The Female Eunuch* (Maidenhead, England: McGraw, 1971; New York: Bantam, 1972). The version of love, marriage, family, etc. which Greer rejects in favor of her rather vaguely defined alternative is an entirely warped version of these things—hardly even resembling the Christian concepts.
3. Num. 11:12; Isa. 49:23.
4. 1 Sam. 1:24; 2:11.
5. Num. 11:12.
6. 1 Thess. 2:11; Eph. 6:4.
7. Prov. 1:8.
8. 1 Tim. 3:4.
9. 1 Tim. 5:14; Mark 14:14; Luke 22:11.
10. Used, e.g., in Plato, *Laws*, 808a. See also Brown, *The New International Dictionary of New Testament Theology*, 2:509; Kittel, *Theological Dictionary of the New Testament*, 2:49; Liddell, *A Greek-English Lexicon*, 2:1203 (none of whom say much!).
11. See Appendix 3 for primary and secondary source references on this, and for Paul's rejection of such low ideas of marriage and of prostitution.
12. Tit. 2:5; see Liddell, *A Greek-English Lexicon*, 2:1205.

13. 1 Cor. 9:19-23.
14. Acts 16:15.
15. Acts 18:3.
16. Acts 18:3, 26.
17. Neh. 3:12.
18. Luke 8:2, 3.
19. Simone de Beauvoir, *The Second Sex* (Drayton, England: Penguin, 1972; New York: Knopf, 1953), p. 449.
20. 1 Tim. 5:14.
21. Gen. 3:19.
22. Ruth 2:2, 3, 8; Prov. 31:16.
23. Eph. 3:10.
24. Gen. 21; 30:15; 1 Sam. 1:6.
25. Matt. 19:9.
26. 1 Cor. 6:15, 16.
27. 1 Cor. 7:4.
28. 1 Cor. 7:7, 8, 26.
29. 1 Tim. 5:14.
30. 1 Cor. 7:33, 34.
31. 1 Cor. 7:36-38, alternate translation.
32. Eph. 6:4.
33. 1 Cor. 7:5.
34. Gen. 1:27.
35. Matt. 23:37.
36. For a popular account see, e.g., Anne Oakley, *Sex, Gender, and Society* (London: M. T. Smith, 1972; New York: Harper and Row, 1973).
37. See, e.g., D. S. Bailey, *Sexual Relation in Christian Thought* (New York: Harper & Bros., 1959), pp. 280, 281.
38. John 11:35; Luke 19:41.
39. Rev. 17:3, 16ff.
40. Eph. 3:10.
41. Gal. 3:28.
42. Matt. 22:30.
43. Rom. 14:23.

Chapter 9
1. Rom. 5:8; 8:35-39; 1 John 4:10.
2. Rom. 3:3; 5:8.
3. John 3:16; 15:13; 1 John 3:17, 18.
4. 2 Cor. 12:14.
5. As in Gal. 2:20.
6. See, e.g., D. Ross Campbell, *How to Really Love Your Child* (Wheaton, Ill.: Victor Books, 1977).

7. Matt. 19:14, 15; Mark 10:13-16.
8. Matt. 10:30.
9. Matt. 6:8; 7:7.
10. Matt. 7:7-11; Luke 11:9-13.
11. Gal. 4:1-7.
12. Luke 15:11-32.
13. John 6:9-13.
14. Matt. 19:13-15; Mark 10:13-15.
15. Matt. 18:2-6; Mark 9:36, 37; Luke 9:47, 48.
16. Matt. 21:15, 16.
17. Luke 2:42, 46.
18. Job 1:8; 2:3.
19. Heb. 12:6.
20. Eph. 6:1, 4.
21. Acts 7:22; 22:3; 2 Tim. 2:25; Tit. 2:12.
22. Discipline = *paideia* (see Brown, *The New International Dictionary of New Testament Theology*, 3:775; Kittel, *Theological Dictionary of the New Testament*, 5:596; Liddell, *A Greek-English Lexicon*, 2:1286), from "teach" in classical usage. Punishment = *ekdikesis* (see Brown, 3:92; Kittel, 2:445; Liddell, 1:504), which concerns justice and avenging wrong.
23. Rom. 13:4; 1 Pet. 2:14.
24. Ps. 103:8-13.
25. Prov. 13:24.
26. Gen. 49:10; Ps. 45:6.
27. Prov. 10:13; 23:13.
28. Ps. 23:4; Mic. 7:14, KJV.
29. Ps. 23:4.
30. Matt. 18:15-19.
31. Eph. 6:4; Col. 3:21.
32. Eph. 4:26.
33. Deut. 6:5-7.
34. 1 Pet. 5:3.
35. John 13:3-5.
36. Eph. 5:1.
37. Ex. 12:26, 27.
38. Prov. 1:8.
39. Luke 15:11-32.
40. Gal. 4:1.
41. Prov. 22:6.
42. Eph. 6:1; Col. 3:20.
43. Luke 2:46.
44. Luke 2:51.
45. Gen. 2:24; Matt. 19:5; Mark 10:7; Eph. 5:31.

46. Matt. 15:4-6; Mark 7:10-12; 1 Tim. 5:4, 16.
47. 2 Cor. 12:14.
48. 2 Sam. 13.
49. 2 Sam. 13:39; 18:33.
50. 2 Sam. 13:22, 26.
51. 2 Sam. 15:1-6.
52. 1 Kings 1:5, 6.
53. 1 Kings 1:6, LXX.

Chapter 10
1. As used in Acts 19:41.
2. 1 Tim. 5:1, 2.
3. Acts 2:46; 20:7-12.
4. 1 Tim. 3:4, 5; 5:17.
5. 1 Cor. 14:37.
6. See Brown, *The New International Dictionary of New Testament Theology*, 1:188; Kittel, *Theological Dictionary of the New Testament*, 2:599; Liddell, *A Greek-English Lexicon*, 1:657; also 1 Pet. 2:25 where *episkopos* is rendered "Guardian" (RSV) or "Overseer" (NIV).
7. See Brown, *The New International Dictionary of New Testament Theology*, 1:192; Kittel, *Theological Dictionary of the New Testament*, 6:651.
8. 1 Tim. 3:1; 5:17 ascribe the same functions. Acts 20:17, 28 directly equate the terms.
9. Acts 14:23; Tit. 1:5.
10. 1 Thess. 5:12; 1 Tim. 3:4, 5; 5:17.
11. 1 Pet. 5:1-4.
12. 1 Tim. 3:2; Tit. 1:7.
13. Psa. 23:4; also Rev. 2:27.
14. Acts 20:28, 29.
15. 1 Tim. 3:2; Tit. 1:9.
16. 1 Tim. 5:17.
17. Matt. 8:19; Mark 4:38; Luke 7:40; John 1:38.
18. Matt. 10:24.
19. Acts 2:42.
20. Tit. 1:9.
21. 1 Pet. 5:1; 2 John 1.
22. Acts 15:6, 22.
23. John 15:27; Acts 1:21, 22; 2:32; 1 Cor. 15:8.
24. 2 Cor. 8:23.
25. E.g., 1 Clement 3:12-16; 19:1-3; 20:22; Ignatius to Rome 2:6; Polycarp to Philippi 2:2.
26. 1 Cor. 14:26.
27. 1 Cor. 14:29.

28. 1 Cor. 14:37.
29. 1 Tim. 2:11, 12.
30. Tit. 2:4.
31. 1 Tim. 2:13-15; see also 1 Cor. 11:8-12.
32. 1 Tim. 2:13; 1 Cor. 11:8, 9.
33. Gen. 2:15-17; 3:9-12.
34. Gen. 3:12.
35. 1 Cor. 11:12.
36. 1 Tim. 2:15, RV.
37. See Rom. 16:20.
38. 1 Tim. 3:1-7.
39. 1 Tim. 3:5.
40. Gen. 2:18; Rom. 16:3; Phil. 4:3.
41. Judg. 4:5.
42. Judg. 2:18.
43. 1 Cor. 14:34. "The Law" probably refers loosely to the Old Testament.
44. Acts 18:26; Rom. 16:3.
45. Rom. 16:1, 2. In one of the earliest extant pagan references to Christianity, Pliny (*Epistles*, x:33, c. A.D. 12) speaks of two female slaves who were "deacons."
46. 1 Chr. 27:31; 29:6; 2 Chr. 8:10; 24:11 (twice).
47. See, e.g., Liddell, *A Greek-English Lexicon*, 2:1526 or any lexicon.
48. In particular, Phil. 1:1; 1 Tim. 3:8.
49. 1 Tim. 3:2-7 (note v. 2); 3:8-13.
50. Acts 6:1, 2.
51. Acts 14:23; Tit. 1:5.
52. Acts 6:3, 5.
53. Acts 6:1.
54. Acts 12:12.
55. Acts 16:15.
56. Col. 4:15. (*Her* house is the preferred reading.)
57. 1 Cor. 1:11.
58. Acts 18:26.
59. 1 Cor. 11:5.
60. For prophecy see Brown, *The New International Dictionary of New Testament Theology*, 3:74-89. Liddell, *A Greek-English Lexicon*, 2:1539 gives classical meaning: "the gift of interpreting the will of the gods."
61. 1 Cor. 14:29.
62. Ex. 15:20; Judg. 4:4; 2 Kings 22:14; 2 Chr. 34:22; Neh. 6:14; Isa. 8:3; Luke 2:36.
63. Joel 2:28; Acts 2:17.
64. Acts 21:9.

NOTES

65. 1 Cor. 14:34.
66. Mishnah Kiddushin 4:13.
67. See, e.g., Popular Judaica Library volume by Hayvim Schneid, *Family* (Philadelphia: Jewish Publications, 1974), p. 88; Strack-Billerbeck, *Kommentar zum Neuen Testament aus Talmud und Midrasch* (Munich: 1922-1928), III:467; Emil Schurer, *A History of the Jewish People in the Time of Jesus* (New York: Schocken, 1961), II:512; and Joachim Jeremias, *Jerusalem in the Time of Jesus* (London: SCM Press, 1973; Philadelphia: Fortress, 1977), p. 374.
68. 1 Cor. 14:35.
69. 1 Cor. 14:37.
70. Eph. 5:19.
71. 1 Cor. 11:21.
72. 1 Cor. 14:27-31.
73. 1 Cor. 14:23, 29-33, 40.
74. 1 Cor. 14:28, 30, 34.
75. 1 Cor. 7:1.
76. 1 Cor. 12:1.
77. Num. 30:9.
78. 1 Cor. 11:10.
79. 1 Cor. 14:29.
80. See Notes 23, 25.
81. Acts 2:42, KJV.
82. Thus 1 Tim. 5:9, which surely cannot refer simply to joining the church.
83. 1 Tim. 2:12.
84. Tit. 2:3, 4.
85. 1 Tim. 2:12, KJV.
86. Ps. 68:11 (see RV, ASV, or any stricter rendering).

Chapter 11

1. Gen. 16:2, 3.
2. Gen. 16:4-6; 21:9.
3. Gen. 21:10.
4. Gen. 21:11, 12.
5. Gen. 16:5.
6. Gen. 16:4, 6.
7. 1 Pet. 3:6.
8. Gen. 21:9.
9. Heb. 11:8-12.
10. Deut. 24:1.
11. Deut. 21:14.
12. Deut. 21:15, 16.
13. Deut. 22:19, 29.

14. 1 Sam. 18:20.
15. 1 Sam. 19:11-18.
16. 1 Sam. 25:42, 43.
17. 1 Sam. 25:44.
18. 2 Sam. 3:15, 16.
19. Deut. 24:4.
20. 2 Sam. 3:13-16.
21. As in 1 Sam. 19:11.
22. 2 Sam. 6:16, 20, 23.
23. 2 Sam. 11.
24. 2 Sam. 12:13.
25. 1 Kings 1:29-35; Deut. 21:15, 16.
26. 2 Sam. 13.
27. 2 Sam. 16:22.
28. 1 Kings 11:1-3.
29. Ezra 10:3.
30. Mal. 2:16.
31. Matt. 19:3.
32. Matt. 19:6; Mark 10:9.
33. Matt. 19:7, 8.
34. Matt. 5:32; 19:9—"fornication" (AV); "unchastity" (RSV); "unfaithfulness" (NIV).
35. For *porneia* (used in Matt. 5:32; 19:9) see Brown, *The New International Dictionary of New Testament Theology*, 2:497; Kittel, *Theological Dictionary of the New Testament*, 6:579.
36. Mark 10:11, 12.
37. See, e.g., John Balsdon, *Roman Women* (London: Bodely Head, 1962; Westport, Conn.: Greenwood, 1975), p. 216.
38. Mark 10:11, 12.
39. Matt. 19:10.
40. Matt. 14:3-11; Mark 6:17-28.
41. Matt. 5:32.
42. Matt. 5:28.
43. Gal. 4:23-26.
44. 1 Pet. 5:1-3.
45. Matt. 5:28.
46. Rom. 3:8.
47. Rom. 7:2; see also 1 Cor. 7:39.
48. Edersheim, *Sketches of Jewish Social Life*, p. 158, ascribes the phrase also to the Rabbis.
49. Matt. 19:6; Mark 10:9. "Separate" is from the Greek verb *korizo*.
50. 1 Cor. 7:10, strictly rendered.
51. 1 Cor. 7:11, strictly rendered.
52. 1 Cor. 7:1.

53. Ezra 10:3.
54. Edersheim, *Sketches of Jewish Social Life*, p. 158; K. E. Keith, *The Social Life of a Jew in the Time of Christ*, p. 84; Mishnah Kethuboth 7:9, 10.
55. See Liddell, *A Greek-English Lexicon*, 1:289, 2:2016, though either *could* be used of marriage breakup.
56. 1 Cor. 7:15.
57. Deut. 24:4.
58. 1 Cor. 7:25-38.
59. 1 Tim. 5:14.
60. 1 Tim. 5:4.
61. See Chapter 5.
62. Eph. 5:28, 29.
63. Matt. 10:37, 38.
64. 1 Cor. 7:32-34.

Chapter 12
1. Mishnah Horayoth 1:4.
2. 1 Cor. 9:5.
3. Matt. 8:14; Mark 1:30; Luke 4:38.
4. 1 Cor. 7:8-40.
5. Eph. 4:1-3.
6. Eph. 3:10.
7. 1 Cor. 7:26.
8. Matt. 24:8; Mark 13:8.
9. 1 Cor. 7:28, 33, 34.
10. 1 Tim. 5:14; cf. 1 Cor. 7:8.
11. Matt. 12:47-50.
12. Col. 1:24.
13. 1 Cor. 7:17.
14. Matt. 19:12.
15. Rom. 7:2.
16. 1 Tim. 5:14.
17. Matt. 22:30; Mark 12:25.
18. Ruth 1:14-17.
19. Acts 13:2; 15:40.
20. 1 Cor. 7:9.
21. Phil. 4:11.
22. John 14:27; Rom. 8:6; Phil. 4:7.

Appendix 1
1. *The Bible and Homosexuality* (London: Gay Christian Movement, 1977); Letha Scanzoni and Virginia Mollenkott, *Is the Homosexual My Neighbor?* (London: SCM Press, 1978; New York: Harper and Row, 1978).

2. Matt. 5:28.
3. Heb. 4:15.
4. Judg. 19 (note "know" in vv. 22, 25).
5. Gen. 19:1-11 (note "know" in vv. 5, 8).
6. Ezek. 16:49, 50.
7. Ecclus. 16:8.
8. Wisdom 19:13, 14.
9. Jude 7.
10. 1 Kings 14:24; 15:12; 22:46.
11. Lev. 18:22; 20:13.
12. Hinted at in *The Bible and Homosexuality*, p. 4.
13. *The Bible and Homosexuality*, p. 8; Scanzoni, *Is the Homosexual My Neighbor?*, pp. 60, 61.
14. Lev. 18:24, 25; 20:23.
15. Gen. 1:31.
16. Gen. 9:3.
17. Mark 7:1-23.
18. 1 Tim. 4:3, 4.
19. Matt. 19:4, 5; Mark 10:6-8.
20. E.g., Eph. 5:31.
21. *The Bible and Homosexuality*, p. 10.
22. *Ibid.;* Scanzoni, *Is the Homosexual My Neighbor?*, p. 77.
23. Scanzoni, *Is the Homosexual My Neighbor?*, p. 77.
24. Rom. 2:14.
25. See above and Romans 3:2.
26. Gen. 2:16.
27. Gen. 1:27.
28. Acts 17:28; Tit. 1:12.
29. E.g., Xenophon's *The Banquet*, and Plato's work of same name.
30. Rom. 1:24-27, RSV, but using the more literal renderings "male" and "female."
31. E.g., Luke 22:15; 1 Tim. 3:1; 1 Pet. 1:12; etc.
32. Scanzoni, *Is the Homosexual My Neighbor?*, p. 62.
33. A famous dictum of Chrysippus, the early Stoic.
34. E.g., Cleanthes and Seneca.
35. Marcus Aurelius, *Meditations*, 4:10.
36. Rom. 8:21, 22.
37. See Note 25.
38. Rom. 1:25; etc.
39. Rom. 1:21.
40. 1 Cor. 6:9; 1 Tim. 1:10.
41. See Brown, *The New International Dictionary of New Testament Theology*, 2:570.

42. E.g., Rom. 9:10; 13:13; Heb. 13:4; and see Brown, *The New International Dictionary of New Testament Theology*, 2:586.
42. Num. 31:17; Judg. 21:12 (LXX).
44. *The Bible and Homosexuality*, p. 3; Scanzoni, *Is the Homosexual My Neighbor?*, p. 66.
45. Scanzoni, *Is the Homosexual My Neighbor?*, p. 67.
46. *The Bible and Homosexuality*, p. 3.
47. Scanzoni, *Is the Homosexual My Neighbor?*, p. 67.
48. *The Bible and Homosexuality*, p. 3.
49. David Field, *The Homosexual Way—A Christian Option?* (Bramcote, England: Grove Books; Downers Grove, Ill.: InterVarsity Press, 1979), p. 22.
50. See Rom. 1:29-31; 1 Cor. 6:9, 10; 1 Tim. 1:9, 10.
51. 2 Tim. 2:22.
52. John 8:11.
53. 1 John 1:9; Heb. 10:22; Matt. 18:22.
54. 1 Cor. 5:1-5; Matt. 18:15-17.
55. Matt. 19:19.
56. Matt. 18:6.
57. Ex. 22:19; Deut. 27:21.
58. Ex. 22:21; Deut. 27:19.
59. Deut. 22:5.

Appendix 2
1. Matt. 15:1-28; 23:25-28; Mark 7:1-30; Rom. 14:14; 1 Cor. 8:8; Col. 2:20-23.
2. 1 Cor. 10:28; Rom. 14:23.
3. Num. 21:9; 2 Kings 18:4.
4. Mark 14:58; Luke 21:5.
5. Mark 7:1-7.
6. Joel 2:28-32; cited in Acts 2:17-21.
7. Rom. 12:3-8; 1 Cor. 12; 1 Pet. 4:10, 11.
8. 1 Cor. 14:26-32.
9. 1 Cor. 12:7.
10. 1 Cor. 11:20-34.
11. Rom. 16:23 (this epistle was written from Corinth); 1 Cor. 7:21.
12. Acts 18:8; 1 Cor. 6:9-11.
13. 1 Cor. 11; for Greek custom see the *Banquets* of Plato, Xenophon, and Athenaeus, and many secondary sources—e.g., Hans Licht, *Sexual Life in Ancient Greece* (Maidenhead, England: Panther, 1969; Westport, Conn.: Greenwood, 1976), p. 57; Leonard Whibley, *A Companion*

to *Greek Studies* (Cambridge, England: University Press, 1931; New York: Hafner, 1963), p. 642.
14. j Meg. 1:12, 72a:53; j. Hor. iii:5; 47d:15; T. Sot. v.9:302; etc.; also 3 Macc. 4:6.
15. Num. 5:18, see also Josephus, *Antiquities*, 3:270 and Susannah 32.
16. 1 Cor. 11:5; cf. v. 3 for pun on "head."
17. Edersheim, *Sketches of Jewish Social Life*, p. 154 cites this, but without reference.
18. Ex. 28:42 (LXX 28:38).
19. See 1 Cor. 11:4; Heb. 10:19, 20.
20. Strack-Billerbeck, *Kommentar zum Neuen Testament aus Talmud und Midrasch*, iii:423-426.
21. See, e.g., Whibley, *A Companion to Greek Studies*, p. 631; Oskar Seyffert, *A Dictionary of Classical Antiquities* (London: Sonneschein & Co., 1891; Magnolia, Mass.: Peter Smith, n.d.), p. 295; Sarah B. Pomeroy, *Goddesses, Whores, Wives and Slaves* (New York: Schocken, 1975), p. 83; and Balsdon, *Roman Women*, p. 257 for equivalent Roman practice.
22. See Note 13.
23. The classes of courtesan are given in, e.g., Lujo Bassermann, *The Oldest Profession* (London: New English Library, 1969; Briarcliff Manor, N.Y.: Stein & Day, 1968), p. 4; Licht, *Sexual Life in Ancient Greece*, p. 332; Fernando Henriques, *Prostitution and Society* (St. Albans, England: McGibbon, 1962; New York: Grove, 1966), p. 53; Whibley, *A Companion to Greek Studies*, p. 614, etc.
24. 1 Cor. 11:10.
25. 1 Cor. 11:5 shows Paul has wives primarily in mind.
26. See, e.g., Hayvim Schneid, *Family*, p. 87.
27. 1 Cor. 11:6.
28. Menander's *Periceiromene*.
29. 1 Cor. 11:16, KJV. The controversial verses 14, 15 may refer to "male pattern baldness" as a physical background to why men with little hair may still be respected elders, while hair is expected on a woman and thus long hair has often become a sexual symbol.
30. See 1 Tim. 3:7; also 1 Cor. 10:32; etc.

Appendix 3

1. E.g., Plato, *Laws*, 781; Aristotle, *Politics*, 1:5. Socrates (see Xenophon, *Symposium*, 1) seems uniquely more enlightened, which may have influenced Plato's hypothetical suggestion of women's education.

2. Attributed (probably spuriously) to Demosthenes in *Ag. Neaeram*, 122.
3. The *hetaera* Aspasia was Pericles' influential mistress; the flute-player Lamia dominated Demetrius. Another *hetaera*, Thais, induced Alexander to burn Xerxes' palace and was later mistress to King Ptolemy, forming the Lagid dynasty. The one-time kings of Cyprus and Pergamum had *hetaerae* for mothers. Women who did rule were *hetaerae* (like Semiramis or Sappho) or descended from them (like Cleopatra).
4. Gen. 16:2; 21:10.
5. Ex. 15:20; Num. 12:1-15; Mic. 6:4.
6. Judg. 4:4.
7. 1 Sam. 1:8, 11.
8. Ruth 4:21.
9. Esth. 5:1; 9:20-32.
10. Talmud Berakoth vii:18, 16.
11. Mishnah Kiddushin 1:7.
12. Mishnah Sotah iii:4.
13. Megillah 23a.
14. Acts 22:3.
15. Gittin 90a.
16. Mishnah Aboth i:5.
17. Mishnah Kiddushin iv:12.
18. Babylonian Talmud Kiddushin 70a, b.
19. Babylonian Talmud Berakoth 43b.
20. Philo, *De Spec Leg*, iii:169.
21. See, e.g., John 3:2 where Jesus is so recognized by a Jewish leader; Acts 22:3.
22. Mark 6:3; Acts 18:3.
23. The most damning exposure of this attitude is in Henry Ibsen, *A Doll's House* (Dayton, England: Penguin, 1965; New York: Dutton, 1954).
24. Dorothy L. Sayers, *Are Women Human?* (Grand Rapids, Mich.: Eerdmans, 1971), p. 47.
25. Luke 11:27, 28.
26. Luke 10:41, 42.
27. John 12:3.
28. Luke 13:19-21; 15:3-10; 18:1-14.
29. Luke 4:25-27; 11:29-32.
30. Matt. 19:29; Mark 7:10, 11; Luke 12:53.
31. Matt. 12:50.
32. Matt. 21:31, KJV.
33. Luke 7:12-16.
34. Luke 8:41ff.

35. Matt. 9:20-22; Lev. 15:25, 27.
36. Matt. 8:14, 15.
37. Luke 13:10-17.
38. Luke 7:37-50.
39. John 8:2-11.
40. Matt. 15:28.
41. Mark 12:43, 44.
42. John 4:9, 27.
43. Luke 1:26-33.
44. Luke 2:36-38.
45. John 4:25, 26.
46. Mark 16:6; John 20:14-17.
47. Luke 8:1-3.
48. Acts 22:3.
49. Aboth i:5; Kiddushin iv:12.
50. Babylonian Talmud Kiddushin 70a, b; Berakoth 43b.
51. Acts 16:13.
52. Acts 16:14.
53. Acts 16:15.
54. Acts 16:15.
55. Acts 12:12; Col. 4:15.
56. Acts 16:40.
57. Rom. 16:1.
58. Prisca, Mary, Junias (probably female); Tryphaena; Tryphosa; Julia; Olympas.
59. Phil. 4:2, 3.
60. Rom. 16:2.
61. Paul K. Jewett, *Man as Male and Female* (Grand Rapids, Mich.: Eerdmans, 1975), p. 132; cf. Brown on women also.
62. *Ibid.*
63. 1 Cor. 13:5.
64. Jewett, *Man as Male and Female,* p. 138, from which a "historical limitation" of Paul's insight is deduced.
65. 1 Cor. 7:21; Eph. 6:5-8.
66. 1 Cor. 7:21.
67. Philemon 16; see also Eph. 6:9.
68. Eph. 5:25.
69. As in 1 Tim. 5:11-14.
70. The literature shows Luther, Calvin, Knox, and more recent men like Hodge and Hendrikson to have made very depreciating comments on women. However, Wesley, Finney, Moody, William Booth, Hudson Taylor, Franson, etc. all accepted women as co-workers and co-preachers.

WORKS CITED OR REFERRED TO

Reference

Brown, Collin, ed. *The New International Dictionary of New Testament Theology,* Vols. 1-3. Exeter, England: Paternoster, 1975-1978; Grand Rapids, Mich.: Zondervan.

Kittel, G., and Friedrich, G., eds. *Theological Dictionary of the New Testament,* Vols. 1-10, London: SCM Press; Grand Rapids, Mich.: Eerdmans, 1964-1977.

Liddell, H. G., and Scott, R., Vols. 1, 2, *A Greek-English Lexicon.* London: Oxford, 1901; New York: Oxford, 1940.

Other

Bailey, D. S. *Sexual Relation in Christian Thought.* New York: Harper & Bros., 1959.

Balsdon, John. *Roman Women.* London: Bodely Head, 1962; Westport, Conn.: Greenwood, 1975.

Bassermann, Lujo. *The Oldest Profession.* London: New English Library, 1969; Briarcliff Manor, N.Y.: Stein & Day, 1968.

Campbell, D. Ross. *How to Really Love Your Child.* Wheaton, Ill.: Victor Books, 1977.

Cotgrove, Stephen. *The Science of Society.* London: Allen & Unwin, 1972, 1978 (U.S.).

de Beauvoir, Simone. *The Second Sex.* Dayton, England: Penguin, 1972; New York: Knopf, 1953.

Edersheim, Alfred. *Sketches of Jewish Social Life.* Grand Rapids, Mich.: Eerdmans, 1974.

Field, David. *The Homosexual Way—A Christian Option?* Bramcote, England: Grove Books; Downers Grove, Ill.: InterVarsity Press, 1979.

Gay Christian Movement. *The Bible and Homosexuality.* London: Gay Christian Movement, 1978.

Greer, Germaine. *The Female Eunuch.* Maidenhead, England: McGraw, 1971; New York: Bantam, 1972.

Henriques, Fernando. *Prostitution and Society.* St. Albans, England: McGibbon, 1962; New York: Grove, 1966.

Ibsen, Henry. *A Doll's House.* Dayton, England: Penguin, 1965; New York: Dutton, 1954.

Jeremias, Joachim. *Jerusalem in the Time of Jesus.* London: SCM Press, 1973; Philadelphia, Fortress, 1977.

Jewett, Paul. *Man as Male and Female.* Grand Rapids, Mich.: Eerdmans, 1975.

Keith, K. E. *The Social Life of a Jew in the Time of Christ.* London: The Church's Mission to the Jews, 1959.
LaHaye, Tim and Beverly. *The Act of Marriage.* Grand Rapids, Mich.: Zondervan, 1976.
Licht, Hans. *Sexual Life in Ancient Greece.* Maidenhead, England: Panther, 1969; Westport, Conn.: Greenwood, 1976.
Miles, Herbert J. *Sexual Understanding Before Marriage.* Grand Rapids, Mich.: Zondervan, 1971.
Oakley, Anne. *Sex, Gender, and Society.* London: M. T. Smith, 1972; New York: Harper and Row, 1973.
Pomeroy, Sarah. *Goddesses, Whores, Wives and Slaves.* New York: Schocken, 1975.
Sayers, Dorothy L. *Are Women Human?* Grand Rapids, Mich.: Eerdmans, 1971.
Scanzoni, Letha, and Mollenkott, Virginia R. *Is the Homosexual My Neighbor?* London: SCM Press, 1978; New York: Harper and Row, 1978.
Schneid, Hayvim, ed. *Family.* Philadelphia: Jewish Publications, 1974.
Schurer, Emil. *A History of the Jewish People in the Time of Jesus.* New York: Schocken, 1961.
Seyffert, Oskar. *A Dictionary of Classical Antiquities.* London: Sonneschein & Co., 1891; Magnolia, Mass.: Peter Smith.
Strack-Billerbeck. *Kommentar zum Neuen Testament aus Talmud und Midrasch.* Munich: 1922-1928.
Whibley, Leonard. *A Companion to Greek Studies.* Cambridge, England: University Press, 1931; New York: Hafner, 1963.
White, John. *Eros Defiled.* Leicester, England: Inter-Varsity Press; Downers Grove, Ill.: InterVarsity Press, 1977.

FURTHER READING

The text of this book attempts to be objective and arose from collaboration (in particular with my previous coauthor Roger T. Forster). But to prepare an objective review of all the literature published on family relationships in the last decade would be an impossible task. It may be helpful, however, to share with the readers the titles of books which I personally found outstanding among the seventy or so I have read on the various topics.

CHRISTIAN BOOKS

Marital adjustment

I have read many Christian books on marital adjustment.

Quite a few, including some very well-known, seemed rather patriarchal and read into Scripture the ideas of their own subculture. Others were better and contained many helpful anecdotes and illustrations. I found none, however, which emerged as clear "first" on this topic, and so will make no recommendation here.

Sex in Marriage

LaHaye, Tim and Beverly. *The Act of Marriage.* Grand Rapids, Mich.: Zondervan, 1976.
As a practical guide to sex (intended for those married or about to be married), this is a clear first choice. It is, however, less useful where it touches on sexual ethics.

Teenage Questions

Stafford, Tim. *A Love Story.* London: Lakeland, 1976; Grand Rapids, Mich.: Zondervan, 1977.
An honest, straightforward, and sensitive book dealing with aspects of courting and sex for teenagers.

Sexual Ethics

White, John. *Eros Defiled.* Leicester, England: Inter-Varsity Press; Downers Grove, Ill.: InterVarsity Press, 1977.
There are several good books available on this topic, but this is my own final choice for those thinking through the issues.

Parenthood

Campbell, D. Ross. *How to Really Love Your Child.* Wheaton, Ill.: Victor Books, 1977.
Some secular experts have called for a removal of restraint and punishment (especially corporal punishment) on children. In reaction to this, some Christian writers advocate a strong inflexible discipline, based on principles of conditioned reflexes, one leading writer actually comparing it to the training of his dog. As Chapter 9 makes clear, I believe this begins from the wrong angle. Teaching personal relationships is not the same as dog training. Campbell seems also to have reacted against the "animal training" school, and his book is my first choice. Care should be taken, however, not to mistake his rejection of rigid conditioning for a rejection of punishment as such. Rather, he is placing it in a more positive disciplinary context.

Other Areas

Three other obvious areas are female identity, being single, and homosexuality. Since I have no personal experience of problems in these areas, it is perhaps imprudent to assess the literature, but of the books read I found none outstanding. Books on general spiritual maturity would also be relevant, but I could not even pretend to make a general recommendation here. On two other areas I might suggest books. One deals well with the qualities of an elder (and so of a good parent):

Getz, Gene. *The Measure of a Man.* Glendale, Calif.: Regal, 1974.

Snyder, Howard A. *The Problem of Wineskins.* Downers Grove, Ill.: Inter-Varsity Press, 1975.

SECULAR BOOKS

There are some areas in which secular literature may usefully supplement our readings.

Childbirth

Leboyer, Frederick. *Birth Without Violence.* London: Fontana; New York: Knopf, 1975.

Wright, Erna. *The New Childbirth.* London: Tandem; New York: Pocket Books, 1971.

Randall, Cher. *Total Preparation for Childbirth.* Plainfield, N.J.: Logos, 1979.

My wife and I were impressed by the ideas of natural childbirth, and our own two children were born using these methods. Dr. Leboyer's book is the classic statement of the ideas. Erna Wright's book was the clearest practical guide we found. Cher Randall's book is a specifically Christian one, though on some medical points its explanation may be a little less clear.

Baby and Child Care

Jolly, Hugh. *Book of Child Care.* London: Sphere, 1977.

Rayner, Claire. *Child Care Made Simple.* London: Allen & Unwin, 1973.

Spock, Benjamin. *Baby and Child Care.* London: Bodley Head; New York: Hawthorn, 1976.

Most parents find it useful to have a general book covering all aspects of baby and child care: physical, medical, psychological, and educational. These three were among those we bought. Jolly and Rayner (the current gurus of English television) were good on physical and medical aspects, as one might expect from a doctor and a nurse. Unfortunately, however, they also contain statements like:

> To hit a small child seems to me to be an admission of failure to understand the child's real needs. I believe it teaches a child to be wary, to lie, to avoid his parents, *not* to obey them; it encourages bullying of younger children, and never really obtains its avowed aim to produce a happy, well-adjusted child.

The recorded experiences of countless Christian parents prove that this is simply untrue, and Christians should unite in opposing such dangerous and unempirical notions. I also disagree with the many secular books which suggest allowing small children to hit each other as a learning process. Dr. Spock's book (a classic with important alterations in emphasis in the second edition) is better on child discipline, but on medical issues seems less well set out.

Early Education

The First Years of Life and *The Pre-school Child.* London: Ward Lock, 1979; Chicago: Follett, 1980.
   Some of the findings of secular psychologists and educationalists are certainly useful in showing us how to encourage and stimulate our children. There are, for example, various popularizations of Piaget which are useful, if taken with an occasional pinch of salt. The books cited above were ones we personally liked best. They were originally written to go with radio and TV programs, but the programs added little to the written material.

Advising Non-Christians

Mace, David and Vera. *Getting Ready for Marriage* and *We Can Have Better Marriages.* London: Oliphants; Nashville: Abingdon, 1972, 1974.
   A secular treatment of marital adjustment will inevitably seem insipid compared with a fully Christian treatment. Sometimes, however, a Christian may have to counsel a couple where one or both have no Christian conviction. The Maces' books might then prove useful.